ENDORSEMENTS

Living, as we do, in an age that faces challenges from the Enlightenment and the realization on the part of many that the ideas of heaven and hell have been used to anesthetize us to the reality of suffering in this world, making us more compliant to the powers of this world, there is much angst over what to make of an afterlife. With a cautious and pastoral approach, Bill Tuck helps us navigate our way through the questions posed by life and death, so that we might journey toward the "undiscovered country" with "quiet confidence and Christian assurance," so that we might approach death with a sense of hope and assurance, while finding encouragement to live this life with boldness and faithfulness.

— Robert Cornwall, Pastor of Central Woodward Christian Church and author of *Faith in the Public Square.*

Bill Tuck is wise enough not to try to give us all the answers to what happens after we die, but he does raise most of the questions, and does it in a way that is thoughtful, imaginative, and open to interesting new possibilities. At almost every point he wonders, "What if it's not the way the preachers have always told us it would be? What if it's different—and better—than we have ever imagined?"

He compares death to birth, and observes how the unborn infant could never know what's waiting for him outside the womb, could never imagine how bright, and beautiful, and full of wonder the world is. But like a twin within that womb, Bill Tuck talks to us about what it might be like, and he talks about it like someone who has given it plenty of thought. He can't be sure. He hasn't been there. But the way he talks about it makes me almost eager to be born, to discover for myself what's waiting beyond the womb of my earthly existence.

— Jim Somerville, Pastor of First Baptist Church Richmond, Virginia

"Many of our fellow Americans seem to live in denial about death, but not William Tuck. He knows that death is not a friend in disguise but an enemy who would destroy us. He is confident that Jesus has defeated death and has promised to share the spoils of his victory with us. His promise gives us hope as we make *The Journey to the Undiscovered Country*. Tuck writes realistically about the second coming of Christ, God's judgment, and hell. His chapter on heaven reinforced my hope and helped me to celebrate what "eye hath not seen, nor ear heard," but which "God hath prepared for them who love him."

This is a beautifully written book and never boring. Tuck knows that many things about the future are mysteries beyond our understanding, so he doesn't speculate unwisely. But neither does he evade difficult questions or disregard the hope-full message of the New Testament. This book is practical and interesting and filled with Christian hope. I recommend it to anyone who wants to face the future realistically and as a Christian. I especially recommend it to those who have arrived at an age where they think regularly about their own mortality."

— Fisher Humphreys, Professor of Divinity emeritus
Samford University, Birmingham, Alabama

"This book is vintage Bill Tuck—thorough research on an important biblical subject, carefully pondered and beautifully illustrated. Chockfull of rich and wonderful nuggets of thought and devotion, it is well worth putting into the hands of anyone who has begun to think about the end of our common trajectory or has already been saddened by the death of a loved one. It is a book to be read, digested, and then read again."

— John Killinger, former Professor & pastor, and author of 70 books including *If Christians Were Really Christians* and *Hidden Mark: Exploring Christianity's Heretical Gospel*.

OTHER BOOKS BY WILLIAM POWELL TUCK

The Way For All Seasons

Facing Grief and Death

The Struggle For Meaning (editor)

*Knowing God: Religious Knowledge
in the Theology of John Baillie*

Our Baptist Tradition

Ministry: An Ecumenical Challenge (editor)

Getting Past the Pain

A Glorious Vision

The Bible As Our Guide For Spiritual Growth (editor)

Authentic Evangelism

The Lord's Prayer Today

Christmas Is for the Young… Whatever Their Age

Through the Eyes of a Child

Love as a Way of Living

The Compelling Faces of Jesus

The Left Behind Fantasy:
The Theology Behind the Left Behind Tales

The Ten Commandments: Their Meaning Today

Facing Life's Ups and Downs

The Church in Today's World

The Church Under the Cross

Modern Shapers of Baptist Thought in America

THE JOURNEY
TO THE
UNDISCOVERED COUNTRY

What's Beyond Death?

William Powell Tuck

Energion Publications
Gonzalez, FL
2012

Cover Design & Original Art: Carol Everhart Roper
carolroper.com

ISBN10: 1-938434-09-9
ISBN13: 978-1-938434-09-9

Library of Congress Control Number: 2012945458

Energion Publications
P. O. Box 841
Gonzalez, FL 32560

energionpubs.com

850-525-3916

To Emily,
my companion through life toward the Celestial City,
whose love, wisdom and gifted insights
have strengthened me along the way

TABLE OF CONTENTS

PREFACE

In one of the churches I served as pastor, a high school student wrote a paper entitled, "The End of Time." He began his paper with this sentence: "This paper will tell and explain about the end of time." That's a remarkable claim for a high school student! But that's the only time I felt I had all of the answers to the Doctrine of the Last Things. When I was in high school, I preached a youth revival in my home church in Lynchburg, Virginia and I spoke with authority on the Second Coming of Christ, Hell and Heaven. I have not been so knowledgeable since!

The theological term for "the last things" is eschatology. Eschatology is the Christian doctrine which is concerned with the final end of humanity. It focuses on matters such as death, the second coming of Christ, the resurrection of the dead, the immortality of the soul, the final judgment, heaven and hell. As I reflected on these topics, I realized that these themes are at the heart of the Christian faith, but it is difficult to voice with clarity what we mean by them.

Although there is no clear, simple, New Testament answer on all of these issues, the New Testament is unequivocal in its hope for men and women in Jesus Christ. No one can speak with certainty about such matters as the mystery of death, the resurrection, heaven and hell, the second coming, or the final judgment of God. However, the New Testament does offer some concrete pointers which I believe can be helpful to us. I invite you to join me as we look to see if we can gain some insight to determine the future hope for those who die in Christ.

The journey toward the "undiscovered country" is filled with uncertainty, puzzling questions, strange reflections and enigmatical images, but it also travels across the bridges, mountains, and valley paths of mystery, faith, hope and anticipation. Let us travel toward our final destination with quiet confidence and Christian assurance.

I want to express a special word of appreciation to Dr. D. E. Ward, MD, who first challenged me to address these themes, and to my wife, Emily, who has dialogued with me about these theological topics and has traveled with me these fifty years toward that Celestial City. I also want to express a special word of appreciation to Linda McNally who proof-read the manuscript for me.

1

The Mystery of Death:
Behind the Veil

Leo Tolstoy recounts a curious Eastern fable which raises puzzling questions. In the story a traveler is attacked and pursued by savage animals, and in an attempt to save himself, he leaps into a dry well and clings to the branch of a wild plant growing on the wall of the well. Looking down he sees a dragon with its jaws wide open ready to devour him if he lets go of the branch. Although his arms are growing weary and he is aware that death awaits him on either side, he stubbornly holds on. Suddenly he notices two mice, one white and the other black, slowly gnawing the stem of the plant to which he is holding. He knows now even more that there is no hope, but suddenly he notices some drops of honey on the leaves of the plant, and he stretches out his tongue and licks them.[1]

Percy Bysshe Shelley says it disquietingly: "Life, like a dome of many-colored glass, stains the white radiance of Eternity, until Death tramples it to fragments." There is no escaping it: death is the absolute question in life. Its insistent inquiry throbs within our heads, burning and twisting for a meaningful response. The Shakespearean query measures the authenticity of existence, "To be or not to be." But who can really conceive of himself or herself as not existing? Unconsciousness, annihilation are fleeting thoughts that run through our minds but are as quickly dismissed as the mind can focus its attention on something else. "Each person is born," so stated Mark Twain, "to one possession which out values all the others-his last breath." Heidegger laid out the direction for other contemporary writers to follow in his influential view that life is primarily a "running forward to death."

We Cannot Escape Death

We cannot escape death; we are caught in its contradictory undertow and we cannot help raising a "why?" Man/woman is a "being unto death"but death remains an annoying enigma which seems to have been savagely injected into the midst of life. Centuries ago Job raised his question, "If a man die, shall he live again?" But there is no if—death is certain. Men and women will die, no one escapes death. There is a thirst within us which will remain eternally unsatisfied if death yanks the cup permanently away from the lips of our desires. We can agree, then, with the apostle Paul, "If for this life only we have hope in Christ, we are of all people most to be pitied" (I Cor. 15:19, NRSV).

Fully aware of the certainty of death, men and women have not been able to shake off the feeling of what George Santayana termed "the soul's invincible surmise." Everywhere and in every age men and women have been convinced that there is more to life than this brown, black, red, gray, yellow, orange clay. There has to be more! In this thought most persons have been unwilling to let go. Is this just wishful thinking, a dread of annihilation, an unrealistic hope, pious nonsense, "pie in the sky" religion, or cowardly behavior? Or – is there any possibility that death is not the end of man's existence? "Death is not a foe," declared Oliver Lodge, "but an inevitable adventure." Milton saw death as "the golden key that opens the palace of eternity." Most persons have lived with this hope.

Most Cultures Affirm Life Beyond Death

From the time of primitive, superstitious caveman to the lunar age, men and women affirmed belief that death is not the end. The Neanderthal man placed hunting and eating items with his dead to indicate his notion of the continuation of life; the Greeks dreamed of the Elysian Fields and the Isles of the Blest; the Egyptian pyramids are lasting monuments of another culture's belief in life after death. The Hebrews pictured life after death as a shadowy existence in Sheol. The American Indian had a vision of a happy hunting ground. The Polynesians saw the moon as their next world while the Mexicans and Peruvians pictured the sun as their future dwelling place. The fierce Norseman looked to his Valhalla; and the Muslim longed for a paradise of sensual satisfaction. In every age and culture men and women have attempted to affirm their belief in life after death.

The primitive expressions, childish notions, fantasized concepts, or worldly depictions may all prove to be inadequate, crude, unsophisticated, antiquated, or even unreal, but this will still not destroy the reality of anticipated life after death. We may have certain ideas or symbols which we use to try to convey our belief in a future beyond the grave, but its existence or nature is in no way determined by our inadequate or puerile descriptions of it. No unborn child could imagine what the world outside the womb would be like; it has no way to make a comparison. No person born blind or deaf can really imagine the wonder of sight and sound. We can project only from our known world, our hopes, our dreams, our aspirations.

Even the Christian, with the revelation he or she has through Jesus Christ, must be cautious in using language about what life after death is like. Paul expressed it vividly: "What no eye has seen, nor ear heard, nor the human heart conceived, what God has prepared for those who love him" (1 Cor. 2:9). Joseph Addison said, "Tis heaven itself that points out an hereafter and intimates eternity to man." Maybe a nineteenth century preacher, Frederick W. Robertson, has said it even better: "Every natural longing has its natural satisfaction. If we thirst, God has created liquids to gratify thirst. If we are susceptible of attachment, there are beings to gratify our love. If we thirst for life and love eternal, it is likely that there are an eternal life and an eternal love to satisfy that craving."[2]

The Mystery of Death

"I just do not understand it, Pastor," the father said to me. "Why did my young son have to die? It just doesn't make any sense to me." Another—"He was only thirty-years-old and a brilliant German professor. Why did he die instead of some useless bum on the street?" Still another—"She was so innocent and young. What did she do to deserve to die, Pastor?" They join the chorus that cries out, "Why?" "Why?" If death is such a natural part of life, then why are we so unsatisfied with the answer that it is just the normal pattern when accidents occur, when cells and organs wear out or malfunction?

Have you had many doctors or ministers describe any death as just the natural thing to expect? If so, why should medical science work so laboriously to fight sickness and prolong life? The answer leaps at us — we sense that death is a contradiction which demands a deeper response. If death is merely a biological event in life, there is no mystery to it, and no darkness would then surround its coming. But for the Christian, death is not simply a physiological fact. "Death proves to be the greatest paradox in the world, which cannot be understood rationally," Berdyaev said. "Death is folly that has become commonplace. The consciousness that death is an ordinary everyday occurrence has dulled our sense of its being irrational and paradoxical."[3]

Helmut Thielicke, a great German theologian and masterful preacher, recounts the following incident from the diary of a young pilot who was shot down in World War II. The pilot was gathering lilacs, and as he parted the branches of a flowering bush he came upon the half-decayed body of a soldier. For someone so young he had witnessed many deaths, and so he drew back in horror, not because he had never seen a dead body before but as a result of the frightful contradiction which he saw between the dead man and the flowering lilac bush. A withered lilac bush would not have horrified him, because he was aware that sooner or later the blooming bush would become a withered bush which is merely an expression of the natural rhythm of life. But the decayed state of the man could not be harmonized with the flowering nature around him. The pilot's recoil reflected his sense that this dead soldier was something contrary to life as God the Creator had planned it. The feeling came over him that the death of man is an unnatural thing. "And this young flier with his shock of horror," observes Thielicke, "was certainly nearer to the world of the New Testament and its message than the people who are always driveling about the 'naturalness' of human death."[4]

The Last Enemy

Heidegger is correct in his assertion that from Paul to Calvin, Christian theology has been written in "the consciousness of death." According to the New Testament teaching, death is the result of sin and is the last enemy to be conquered. The apostle Paul declared: "The wages of sin is death" (Rom. 6:23). "The sting of death is sin" (1 Cor. 15:56). "Therefore as sin came into the world through one man and death through sin, and so death spread to all men because all men sinned" (Rom. 5:12). "The last enemy to be destroyed is death" (1 Cor. 15:26). Death is seen, then, from the biblical perspective not merely as a biological fact, but it is seen primarily as a moral fact.

Death is an enemy; it is not a part of order but disorder. Sin is the Christian way of explaining the reality of death. Sin is seen as human rebellion against the source of our very being, God. This rebellion results in separation from God, outside of whom is only death. It results also in our separation from our loved ones by death. This linking of death with sin seems to go against the grain of modern society and sounds like some ancient mythological way of speaking which should be forgotten and dismissed. Before you cast it aside, however, look first at what you may be surrendering. Let's see if we can determine where the biblical writers were heading with such a strange sounding doctrine.

The Soul

"Death is so final," we often say, and the Christian faith teaches finality about it that is even more threatening than some have been willing to accept. Many religions, especially the ancient Greek view of immortality, have at the center of their concept of death the idea that there is something within men and women, a divine spark or something akin to it, which never dies but continues after the physical body dies. But this is not so in the Christian faith. The Old and New Testaments affirm strongly the unity man/woman-body, mind and spirit-and when man/woman dies the destruction is total and complete.

Men and women, as understood in the biblical sense, do not have a soul which departs from the body at death, but man/woman is a soul (Gen. 2:7). Many of the ancient Greeks despised the body and viewed one's body as a prison or a tomb which contained the soul. The body itself was seen as evil and the soul finally found release in its confinement at death. In contrast to this view, the New Testament focuses on the salvation of the whole person and not just the soul. When a person dies, all of that person dies, not just the body, and salvation is concerned with the whole person and not just a part the person called a soul. The New Testament writers were aware that flesh and blood cannot inherit the kingdom of God. They spoke of the resurrection of the body as the act of God who would recreate and glorify the body so the perishable was transformed into the imperishable.

Among some of the ancient Greek thinkers, the soul was de-picted as a spark from God which had entered into the body of persons. The death of the body freed the soul so that it could be absorbed once again into God's being. But this absorption, how-ever, meant the loss of person-hood and individuality for men and women. The New Testament emphasis on the resurrection of the body is the biblical way of expressing the idea that the personality of men and women is not obliterated at death but that the individual personality of each believer survives death. This survival will be in the form of a glorified, transformed, spiritual body, which will be imperishable and incorruptible (1 Cor. 15:35-54; 2 Cor. 5:18).

Death is both a challenge and a threat to the total person. Like the child's jingle says:

> *I had a little dog*
> > *His name was Rover,*
> *When he lived,*
> > *He lived on clover,*
> *When he died,*
> > *He died all over.*

Resurrection

Some preachers have used the awesome finality of death as a means of persuading people to come to Jesus for redemption before it is "too late." Albert Schweitzer, in a sermon delivered at St. Nicolai's Church, noted that in the past it was considered Christian to use people's fear of death in order to frighten them into believing in eternal life. He tells about a famous chaplain in a French king's court who would point from his pulpit to the vaults where the nobility were buried along the wall of the royal chapel and describe how those who were now dead used to sit in the chapel, dressed in their finery, full of life and gaiety, and listened to his voice as those present were now doing. He then painted a gruesome picture, describing the past royalty as now buried, decaying, and rotting away. After this awful description, he believed his listeners were now ready to hear a sermon on repentance and eternal life.

"But what had he preached to them?" Schweitzer asked. "The sovereignty of death. Where there is terror and fear of death, there death reigns."[5] The Christian faith, however, does not want to propose "the sovereignty of death" but it declares that Christ died to "deliver all those who through fear of death were subject to lifelong bondage" (Heb. 2:15).

If we were able to solve the riddle about death, then all other questions would become secondary. In the biblical concept, death is not merely the last moment of life but it is "the last enemy to be destroyed" (1 Cor. 15:26). The New Testament answer to the mystery of death is a strange word: resurrection. Death, as a part of the total mystery of life, does not have the final word to say about human existence; the ultimate word has been declared in the resurrection of Jesus Christ. The New Testament resounds with this sense of exultation, and nowhere is it more clearly evident than in I Corinthians 15. Listen to Paul as he shouts a victory cry:

> Death is swallowed up in victory.
> O death, where is thy victory?
> O death, where is thy sting?
> The sting of death is sin, and the
>   power of sin is the law.
> But thanks be to God, who gives us the
>   victory through our Lord Jesus Christ
> (1 Cor. 15:55-56).

"But wait a minute," modern men and women want to say. "The word resurrection doesn't help much. Resurrection sounds offensive and unreal in this Space Age." Why do modern men and women assume they are any different in their reaction to this word than ancient persons? Paul had the attention of the crowd of Athenians at Areopagus until he uttered the strange word, resurrection, and then most of them jeered and walked away. No, the ancient mind found the word as unpalatable as contemporary, urban men and women do. The Stoics insisted that men and women should learn to face death bravely as the natural biological conclusion to one's existence. The Epicureans laughed and said: "Live life to the fullest in this life, since there is nothing after death, no harm can come to you, then, eat, drink and be merry for tomorrow we die." Even the Hebrew mind, except for a few fleeting insights, noted in Psalms 16:8-11; 73:21-26; Job 19:24-27; Isaiah 26:19; and Daniel 12:23, conceived of life after death as only a shadowy sort of existence in Sheol.

Life After Death

A strong belief in life after death did not become a vital part of the Hebrew belief until during what is usually called the inter-biblical period, that time between the last written document of the Old Testament and the New when the Jewish nation came greatly under the influence of Persian philosophy. To the Greek mind the notion of resurrection was appalling; man/woman had an immortal soul, and at the time of death the divine soul flew from the body which had been its prison to give it full release to return to heaven. Ancient thoughts about death and the possibility of life beyond it closely parallel **the** pattern of secular, urban persons: skepticism, agnosticism, unbelief, stoic acceptance, death as a natural process, and a belief by some few in the immortality of the soul.

Death is a mystery, yes, but so is resurrection. But this latter mystery is set forth by the church to answer the former. The problem of death is central to the Christian faith, because the awesome reality and dimension of sin are taken with genuine seriousness. Adam, every person, has fallen; he or she has chosen the way of death, the path of sin estrangement from God, his or her fellow man, and even his or her authentic self. The New Testament posits incarnation, cross, redemption, atonement, salvation, and resurrection to remove the barriers of sin, evil, fragmentation, lost-ness, and death. Sin is costly; it results in death. The New Testament "good news," the gospel, lifts up the cross-resurrection as God's answer to the tragedy of sin-death.

Perhaps our difficulty in understanding the New Testament's ringing assurance in the resurrection is that we have not taken seriously enough the terrible nature of sin. Paul reminded the Corinthian church about the nature of the gospel he first preached to them: "For I delivered to you as of first importance what I also received, that Christ died for our sins. . . that he was buried, that he was raised on the third day" (1 Cor. 15:34). Again, Paul declared forcefully:

If we have been united with him in a death like his,
we shall certainly be united with him in a resurrection
like his. We know that our old self was crucified with
him so that the sinful body might be destroyed, and we
might no longer be enslaved to sin. For he who has died
is freed from sin. But if we have died with Christ, we
believe that we shall also live with him. For we know that
Christ being raised from the dead will never die again;
death no longer has dominion over him. The death he
died he died to sin, once and for all, but the life he lives
he lives to God. So you also must consider yourself dead
to sin and alive to God in Christ Jesus (Rom. 6:5-11).

"For whatever is truly wondrous and fearful in man, never yet
was put into words or books," wrote Herman Melville. "And the
drawing near of Death, which alike levels all, alike impresses all
with a last revelation, which only an author from the dead could
adequately tell." Isn't this the claim of the church? One from the
dead has returned to share with us his revelation, his victory, Jesus Christ, the living Lord. According to the New Testament, the
foundation stone upon which the Christian church is built, is the
resurrection of Jesus Christ.

Let us focus on the significance which the resurrection of Jesus has for our faith and the light it may shed on the mystery of
death. The New Testament discussion of the resurrection of Jesus
revolves around at least three great affirmations about Christ, God,
and man.

Death and the Resurrection of Jesus

"Christianity stands or falls with the reality of the raising of
Jesus; from the dead by God," so declares contemporary theologian Jürgen Moltmann. "In the New Testament there is no faith
that does not start *a priori* with the resurrection of Jesus." [6] "In the
resurrection of Jesus," another contemporary theologian, Wolfhart
Pannenberg, states: "We therefore have to do with the sustain-

ing foundation of the Christian faith. If this collapses, so does everything else which the Christian faith acknowledges."[7] Gerd Lüdemann, a German New Testament scholar, affirms that "the resurrection of Jesus is the central point of the Christian religion."[8]

The apostle Paul pointed in the same direction when he argued: "If Christ has not been raised, your faith is still futile and you are still in your sins" (1 Cor. 15:17). The resurrection was not a secondary or debatable matter with Paul; if it fell, the whole house of faith collapsed with it; if it proved false, nothing else mattered. It was the one essential truth on which, he believed, all the rest of the faith depended—salvation, forgiveness, reconciliation, and hope for life beyond the grave.

Paul, along with the other writers of the New Testament, was aware that what Jesus is stands for more than what he said. Paul had the emphasis in the right place when he spoke of the risen Christ and not the Sermon on the Mount. The ethical and moral teachings of Jesus are important and should not be minimized, but the vitality of all his teachings take on a new dimension in light of the resurrection. He died as he had taught men and women to live, self-sacrificially; however, without the resurrection the cross would have marked the tragic end to the life of a good and wise young teacher. The resurrection is a confirmation of the incarnation, "that God was in Christ reconciling the world unto himself."

Resurrection affirms that Jesus was who he said he was; that what he said was from one who had the authority to say it, and that, in approval of a life lived and laid down for the sin of man, God raised Jesus up. "A Christian faith that is not resurrection faith," Moltmann says, "can therefore be called neither Christian nor faith. It is the knowledge of the risen Lord and the confession to him who raised him that form the basis on which the memory of the life, work, sufferings and death of Jesus is kept alive and presented in the gospels."[9]

Saturday's Children

Many today are still living on the wrong side of the Easter event. They are caught in the middle between Friday and Easter Sunday. They have stopped after the crucifixion and remained on Saturday in despair. They have become Saturday's children. Saturday's child is caught between the Friday of death and the Sunday of resurrection. She has not moved to the dawn of hope, so she still dwells in despair, fear, meaninglessness, and defeat. Can you imagine what that Saturday must have been like to the disciples of Jesus after his horrible crucifixion? Look and listen for a moment to the disciples as they may have gathered together in the upper room. Their faces are drawn and saddened by the events; their eyes are darkened from want of sleep; despair fills their hearts and minds. The vision of the messianic kingdom seems defeated. Peter decides to return to his old job of fishing. Where would the others go? Could Matthew collect taxes again? What could they do now? The blush of shame is still felt in the faces of some. Peter can never forget his denial of his Lord in the courtyard, "I never knew him." Disciples who said they were fortified to "drink his cup" and would never forsake him had fled to safety when danger appeared. Only the women and John stayed near the cross. Fear also filled their eyes. The door was bolted shut; they were afraid that the Roman or religious authorities who had put Jesus to death might be looking for them now.

There they huddled on Saturday, hearts broken with despair, minds tormented with fright, bodies weary from sleepless exhaustion, spirits tormented with defeat and their dreams shattered. They were Saturday's children with a long way to go, but on Sunday morning the dawn of a new hope broke upon them - the resurrection of Jesus. They had not looked for it; had not expected it; could hardly believe it. But once the light of that resurrection morning began to shatter the darkness of their despair, a faith, joy, and hope unfolded which turned defeat to victory, tears to laughter, sadness to joy, tragedy to hope, despair to celebration, cowardliness to courage, faithlessness to commitment, and disciples to apostles. An unbelievable event had taken place.

The resurrection is a unique event as an act of God which transcends history, and it summons men and women to a radical commitment of faith to a living Lord. "If you confess with your lips that Jesus is Lord and believe in your heart that God raised him from the dead, you will be saved" (Rom. 10:9).

The Manner in Which Jesus Faced Death

We sometimes too quickly or too easily forget the manner in which Christ himself faced the prospect of his own death. "When they reached a place called Gethsemane, he said to his disciples, 'Sit here while I pray.' And he took Peter and James and John with him. Horror and dismay came over him, and he said to them, 'My heart is ready to break with grief; stop here, and stay awake.' Then he went forward a little, threw himself on the ground, and prayed that, if it were possible, this hour might pass him by" (Mark 14:32-35, NEB). Some have dismissed Jesus' fear of death as merely the awesome spiritual agony he knew he had to face, but others have observed in his response the normal reaction that all humanity senses in the realization of approaching death. His peace came later as he emerged from Gethsemane armed with a sense of God's will and grace.

As Jesus faced the dark enigma of death, he walked as we walk by faith—with the same feelings, frustrations, hopes, fears and emotions—but in his faith he moved with a vital awareness of the trustworthiness, reliability and presence of God. Carlyle Marney is right; Jesus "faithed" his way through death just as we must do, and he had no "life back guarantee," but he "bet his life" on the Father he served.

In Jesus Christ we see Adam, man/woman, as he/she was meant to be—not partial, not fragmented, not incomplete but whole, full, complete man or woman. "God cuts through the strands of human history in an incarnation, an enfleshing," Marney says, "to make a demonstration of what man is like when he is completed. God's idea, his realized demonstration, is Jesus Christ, Redeemer, Son of God, *monogones* (only one of its kind), who invades history as its Master and finished product not only to demonstrate but to make completion possible."[10] As the new Adam, Jesus Christ, who has been raised from the dead, then becomes "the first fruits of those who have fallen asleep" (I Cor. 15:20). He is also "the faithful witness, the firstborn of the dead" (Rev. 1:5). The Christian has hope in the face of death because he puts his trust in the same power which brought life to him in the beginning, Jesus Christ.

Our hope for life after death is based on the resurrection of Jesus Christ from the dead. Any continuity for life after death is grounded in a power outside ourselves, the power of God who alone is able to raise the dead. "If Christ has not been raised," Paul asserts, "your faith is futile and you are still in your sins" (1 Cor. 15:17). But our faith is: "because he lives, we shall live also." "I am the resurrection and the life; he who believes in me, though he die, yet shall he live, and whoever lives and believes in me shall never die" (John 11:25).

Death and the Nature of God

The "whys" surrounding death will not cease their relentless inquiry easily. For many they reach all the way into the very presence of God. Some simply say softly, "I'll ask God one day and God will explain all." Others will have none of it. They cry out bitterly: "If God cares; if God is so loving, why did she die? I just do not understand it!" Some are bold enough to assert that man and woman's death raises a moral question directed at the very nature of God. "Fundamentally man's death appears to indict the Creator," says New Testament scholar, Leander E. Keck, "for it raises the question, How did it happen that the undying Creator made life subject to death?"[11]

This question lifts out the central problem death poses questions about the very integrity of God. But the New Testament pushes the pointer around the other way and focuses the blame not on God but on men and women. Some would like to dismiss the Genesis story of the Fall as mere ancient mythology, but no matter how you size up the account, Adam, every man, rebels from God's fellowship by his free choice, not by God's rejection. Man turns from God, not God from man. The conclusion is something we may not like, but it is unavoidable the New Testament links death with human sin. Our sin, we must admit, is real. Few have expressed it as well as the late theologian Paul Tillich:

> Thus the state of our whole life is estrangement from others and ourselves, because we are estranged from the Ground of our being, because we are estranged from the origin and aim of our life. And we do not know where we have come from, or where we are going. We are separated from the mystery, the depth, and the greatness of our existence. We hear the voice of that depth; but our ears are closed. We feel that something radical, total, and unconditioned is demanded of us; but we rebel against it, try to escape its urgency, and will not accept its promise.[12]

Death Does Not Sever Our Connection With God

Without question, our knowledge of our own certain demise is entangled with an understanding of the character of God. That should not cause despair; it is the ground for confident hope. In the middle of an argument with the religious sect called the Sadducees, who did not believe in the resurrection of the dead, Jesus pointed them to the Pentateuch, the only section of the Old Testament Scriptures which they accepted as authentic. There he confronted them with their own Scriptures. "And as for the dead being raised, have you not read in the book of Moses, in the passage about the bush, how God said to him, 'I am the God of Abraham, and the God of Isaac, and the God of Jacob'? He is not God of the dead, but of the living; you are quite wrong" (Mark 12:26-27). What has that got to do with resurrection? Everything! The implication and declaration of Jesus is that Abraham, Isaac, and Jacob are still living in a vital relationship to God, even death has not severed the tie which bound them to him.

Here, then, is the real lesson about the integrity and character of the God of the universe: God does not blow out the personality of men and women as if it were a dime store candle; God has not placed in our hearts a quest for the eternal to turn around and snatch it from our grasp; God has not created us in the divine image whimsically to toss us aside as valueless; God has not planted this restlessness within us to extinguish it without a sense of fulfillment. As Jesus told the Sadducees, we do not know the Scriptures nor the power of God.

The nature and character of God are evidences of the assurance we can have that God will not cast aside his creation but will sustain a vital relationship with it. What God has started with us, God will finish. We are yet incomplete but God is pulling us toward completion. We are not yet as much as what we can be—long to be-hope to be—should be—can be—but it is God's power which will enable us to become. When God looked upon the whole creation, even men and women or maybe especially men and women, God did not say that it was perfect or complete; "And God saw everything that he had made and behold, it was very good" (Gen. 1:31).

Nature Is Incomplete

Paul was willing to push the mystery beyond human beings to nature itself. It, too, is incomplete, not fulfilled. Why is there so much tragedy even within nature's "angry red claw"? Do the little fish and small animals exist only to be devoured by the larger creatures? "A veil of sadness is spread over all nature," Schelling said, "a deep unappeasable melancholy over all life." Nature's tragedy is linked with humankind, Paul was bold to assert:

For the creation waits with eager longing for the revealing of the sons of God; for the creation was subjected to futility, not of its own will but by the will of him who subjected it in hope; because the creation itself will be set free from its bondage to decay and obtain the glorious liberty of the children of God. We know that the whole creation has been groaning in travail together until now; and not only the creation, but we ourselves, who have the first fruits of the Spirit, groan inwardly as we wait for adoption as sons, the redemption of our bodies (Rom. 8:19-23).

Men and women are apart from nature and yet are a part of nature. Human beings and nature are tied together in a web of life. As we move toward atonement with God, so the natural order seeks its atonement. There is a solidarity not only which we share with all humanity but which we bear with all living things. The ecologists have warned us what our pollution and wasteful style of life have already unleashed upon the world. Lewis Mumford stated our dilemma when he wrote: "Though he is now the dominant species, his fate is still bound up with the prosperity of all forms of life."[13] Natural as well as moral laws of the universe have been violated by man and the redemptive process is concerned not only with us but with all creation which is itself moving toward fulfillment. "The tragedy of nature," Tillich observes, "is bound to the tragedy of man, as the salvation of nature is dependent on the salvation of man."[14] Tied together by a chord that will not fully free one without the other, human beings and nature move toward the completeness which God has created them to have. Douglas John Hall, Professor of Theology at McGill University in Montreal, declares that "redemption, as it is glimpsed in Jesus Christ, has a cosmic and not only a human dimension. It is to insist that resurrection- not immortality, but resurrection- applies to the whole created order. . ."[15]

I have to confess that I cannot understand very clearly the frightful hold sin has on us and the world nor the way God's power shatters its grip and sets us free. It's tough trying to understand talk about redemption of men and women, much less nature, but I am also struck by the limited and partial nature of any knowledge which I might have.

When my twin grandchildren were three-years-old, they were not able yet to grasp the meaning of many multi-syllable words I might be able to read, but that did not lessen my love for them nor my intention of guiding them into deeper knowledge. Their limited knowledge did not mean that I could not have a meaningful relationship with them which would deepen and enrich our love, compassion, and understanding. Just because their knowledge was limited and their perspective was childish did not mean that they could not know me, love me, and respond to me. They could and do.

My knowledge of God, from God's perspective, in fact from any, must seem so childish, immature, primitive, limited, narrow, and confining, but this does not mean that I cannot have some knowledge and live and act on the basis of the partial knowledge of God which I do have. I am certain that as the Father, God is seeking to guide me into deep insights.

Our knowledge of God is limited but that we can know God, at least partially, is a Christian certainty. Once when a traveler became lost in the hills of Tennessee, he stopped at a small crossroads store and asked an old gentleman where Knoxville was. "I don't know, Mister," the old man replied, "where Knoxville is, 'cause I've never been there, but there's the road to it." Our knowledge of God, like the old man's knowledge of Knoxville, may be limited and partial, but we know the way. Jesus Christ, himself, has made the way clear and now we seek to walk in it. We have become "men and women of the way."

Death and the Nature of Humanity

The question of the psalmist is echoed through the centuries. "What are human beings, that you are mindful of them, mortals that you care for them?" (Ps. 8:4 NRSV). Who and what is this man-woman creature? He/she is an enigma. He or she loves and hates; he or she is kind and cruel; he or she is brave and cowardly; he or she is understanding and judgmental; he or she is compassionate and mean. With one hand a man reaches out to lift up a fallen companion; the other hand pulls a trigger to take a life. A strong arm helps a weary traveler; the other pulls a lever to knock down a building. With strong legs men and women scale a mountain or block the path of another person moving toward freedom.

With one's mind, a person can focus his or her attention to think the thoughts of God after God or plan diabolical ways of destroying the human race. Who is man/woman? He/she is a menagerie. He/she wants to be Prometheus; Superman, to be a god. He/she wants to rule the land, the sea, and the air. His or her greatest sin is "God almighty-ness."

There is an inseparable link between sin and death, so that death follows from sin. According to Emil Brunner:

> Sin is not merely moral evil, but the rebellion of the creature against the Creator. When man as sinner denies his dependence on God and turns it into independence, he is severed from God the original source of all life; his guilt stands between the living God and himself as he actually is. Then the creature destroys the rest of its own life, its fellowship with God.[16]

In Jesus Christ we see the New Adam—man as he should be—related fully to the Source of life. "For there is one God, and there is one mediator between God and men, the man Christ Jesus" (I Tim. 2:5). I like Frank Stagg's way of understanding the title of mediator as applied to Jesus Christ. He sees mediator as meaning more than someone who is between God and humankind. "Jesus came to overcome the between-ness between God and man."[17] In Jesus Christ we are able to have a deeper look into the nature of both God and human beings.

Some people have been content to depict human beings as animals and no more. Others see human beings as complicated machines, while another describes human beings as accidents of fate whose lives are without purpose or meaning. On the other hand, the biblical picture of men and women presents us as creatures who have been created in the image of God (Gen. 1:26-27; 1 Cor. 11:7). The creation of the image of God within human beings was God's way of endowing us with some measure of God's own personal nature. Because we have been created in the image of God, it is possible for us to have communion with God. This fact indicates the eternal significance which God has given to human personality.

"Whatever the doubtful phrase, 'the image of God' may mean," states H. Wheeler Robinson, "it is certainly intended to recognize man's unique relation to God, and his supremacy over the animal world."[18] God's revealing love was not given to inanimate rocks and water but to human beings; it is person to person. We are what we are because God created us different from the dust of the ground, animals, or plants; we were created to have fellowship with God. God has given to human beings the gift of self-conscious reason, and this is distinctive of persons alone of all of creation. Human beings share in the nature of God by God's creative act.

Man's and woman's rebellion against God is taken very seriously by God. The "wages of sin is death," but God loves us too much not to seek restoration. The coming of the "Word . . . made flesh" shows the supreme worth God maintains for his creation. God continually wants to preserve the unique personality of human beings both in this life and the life after death. If persons were not significant to God, the incarnation would not have happened in the first place. Maybe this is the reason some people still reject the incarnation today; their opinion of persons is too low. He or she is not worth redeeming.

As Christians, we should not give in to despair or hopelessness because of our sins or suffering, but remember that ultimately we affirm our faith in God's grace and love and that death is not the end but a new beginning. However, this belief is based on trust, not scientific knowledge. Douglas John Hall states that "we are being given the grace to become the creatures that we are; to trust the Lord and Giver of life in place of the futile attempt to possess life."[19] Jürgen Moltmann reminds us that this hope is based on trust.

> The immortality of the soul is an opinion- the resurrection of the dead is a hope. The first is a trust in something immortal in the human being, the second is trust in the God who calls into being the things that are

not, and makes the dead live. In trust in the immortal soul we accept death, and in a sense anticipate it. In trust in the life-creating God we await the conquest of death- 'death is swallowed up in victory' (I Cor. 15:54)- and eternal life in which 'death shall be no more' (Rev. 21:4).[20]

God's grace and love in Jesus Christ reveal the lengths to which God will go to bring human beings back into fellowship. For this reason, it seems impossible to accept talk of the annihilation and extinction of human personality at death as having any plausible grounds on which to stand. Many contemporary writers have given way to a spirit of hopelessness which has begun to overwhelm the outlook of men and women. John Baillie maintains, however, that the Christian does have hope and a hope not only in his present existence but in the life to come after death. The Christian's hope is based on his personal knowledge of the eternal God and is rooted in our continuous religious fellowship with the eternal God. Our hope of eternal life issues out of our awareness that we can have knowledge of God in communion with God. The only unanswerable argument for life after death, Baillie believes, is realized in the fact that God is the God of individuals who can enter into fellowship with him. Baillie sets forth what he calls a "logic of hope." "If the individual can commune with God, then he must matter to God; and if he matters to God, he must share God's eternity."[21]

The Christian hope of eternal life is grounded in our fellowship with God.

Eternal Life as Present and Future

Many of us have difficulty understanding the concept of resurrection for the Christian because it seems to suggest both that it is something to be realized in the distant future and that it is also a present possession of the believer. One needs to be honest and admit that the New Testament contains descriptions of both viewpoints. The concept of a future consummation is depicted in

1 Thessalonians 4 and I Corinthians 15:52-58, along with other passages, where Paul says that those who are dead will be awakened at the return of Christ with a cry from the archangel and the sound of the trumpet of God. Romans 8 speaks even of a future cosmic redemption of both man and nature.

At the same time Paul says that he was eager to "depart and be with Christ" (Phil. 1:23) at the time of death and that "the old had already passed away and that the new had already come and that everyone in Christ was already a new creation" (2 Cor. 5:17). Many other places could be suggested to show the varying descriptions of what the resurrected life is to be like. Is there any way to reconcile the two? Can resurrection be both present and future?

Stagg has looked at this apparent contradiction and concluded: "What appears to be a time interval to us who are bound by time may be no interval at all to God or to those who through death have entered into eternity with him. The resurrection which is future to those within time may be present reality to those who have died and who are now with the Lord in a bodily state."[22] Brunner has expressed it well. "The date of death differs for each man for the day of death belongs to this world. Our day of resurrection is the same for all and yet is not separated from the day of death by intervals of centuries for these time intervals are here not there in the presence of God, where 'a thousand years are as a day.'"[23] In some sense God, to whom one day is "as a thousand years, and a thousand years as one day" (2 Pet. 3:8), transcends time and relates his eternal life for us both as a present possession and a future reality.

Eternal life for the Christian is not merely something which begins when we die but is a dimension of existence in which we begin here and now. The resurrection of Jesus Christ marks the coming of the new age, and now the church proclaims that through Christ's death and resurrection forgiveness of sin and new life are available to persons of faith. The message, however, is that the new life is a present possession of the believer which begins with trust. "And this is eternal life, that they know thee the only true God, and Jesus Christ whom thou hast sent" (John 17:3. See also 2 Cor. 4:10-11; 1 John 4:9).

The Christian faith notes the awesome seriousness of death and does not see persons as having some part, or spark, or soul, or spirit that can depart from one's body without death touching it. We are a unit; and a whole person, and we do not possess a soul; each of us is a soul. When we die biologically we die totally, and each of us is then raised by God as a "spiritual body," transformed, imperishable, glorified, and with power, to be like the last Adam, Christ, our Lord (1 Cor. 15:44-57). The New Testament does not maintain that we will have the same physical body, but like a grain of wheat, Paul says, it will be changed, but we will not lose our own identity or uniqueness (Phil. 3:21; Acts 17:31).

The New Testament, especially the Gospel of John, does not make a distinction between the time of this world and the time of the realm where one lives after death. In fact, John's Gospel states that eternal life is a present possession of the Christian; it transforms the present and makes one aware of living in eternity now. Through Christ even the time barrier has been overcome. To know God through his Son is to possess eternal life now.

The Greek word for eternal is not concerned so much with length of life but with the quality of life. Eternal life is the life of God and through an intimate, personal relationship, which Christ has made available, we can participate here and now in the eternal life of God. Even death itself cannot destroy this relationship. "Truly, truly, I say to you, he who believes has eternal life" (John 6:47). God's time is eternity and God is the only one "from everlasting to everlasting" (Ps. 90:2); "the same yesterday and today and for ever" (Heb. 13:8); He is the "Alpha and Omega, . . . which is, and which is to come, the Almighty" (Rev. 1:8, KJV). The one who has initiated the new creation is the one the Scriptures declare was with God "in the beginning" (John 1:1). The Lord over time has given persons who live in time an opportunity to share in eternity through fellowship with him. God's love has reached out to human beings before the "foundation of the world" (John 17:24; Rev.

13:8). God's eternal love is boundless, and it stretches back beyond history and forward into the fulfillment of time.

Peering Behind the Veil

Many methods have been used to try to peer behind the veil of death to see if anything is there. In their quest, men and women have attempted to read the stars, tea leaves, palms, crystal balls, and cards; they have listened to mediums who allegedly talk with the dead; some have even dreamed of "time machines" which would carry a person into the future and beyond. Few have found much lasting satisfaction through these paths. For many, life seems to be heading for a dead-end street. The grave seems to pronounce a final word of defeat to the meaning and purpose of life. The New Testament, however, is bold to assert that the decisive victory over sin and death has already been won through the life, death, and resurrection of Jesus Christ. "D day" has already come! The war may continue for some time yet, but the decisive battle has already been accomplished through Christ's victory over the grave.

The last book in the Bible relates the victory cry as the seer of Patmos records his vision of the living Christ. "Behold I am alive for evermore, and I have the keys of Death and Hades" (Rev. 1:18). The Christian hope rings through the centuries in the words of Jesus to Martha: "I am the resurrection and the life; he who believes in me, though he die, yet shall he live, and whoever lives and believes in me shall never die" (John 11:25-26).

The complete mystery of death is never fully removed, but the Christian seeks to meet it as Lord Balfour did when he closed his eyes in death and whispered, "This is going to be a great experience." Life is a great gift; we rejoice in it and want to use this great gift to the fullest of our capacity. We are reminded, however, by Schweitzer's interpretation of the apostle Paul that we know that this world is "a house sold for the breaking up" and so we will live in it with care; but we will not invest our entire holdings in it.

A person can die, or he or she can die in Jesus Christ. We can die as only a biological creature, or we can die as children of nature and children of God. At the moment of death, we are absolutely dependent upon faith. At this critical moment, all else fails us wealth, pride, prestige, power, influence, friends. The only available resource for us is faith in God. Here in this moment, as in no other, we must acknowledge an absolute dependence on the power of God. Our power is totally diminished-we are wholly dependent on the Holy One.

Death Is the Last Enemy

The Christian approaches death with the awareness that "the last enemy to be destroyed is death." Death is not our "natural" end but is an enemy of God and stands in opposition to God's ultimate will. "Death is the peak of all that is contrary to God in the world, the last enemy," says Karl Barth, "thus not the natural lot of man, not an unalterable divine dispensation."[24] But Jesus Christ has already won the battle against death and so Paul can shout: "Thanks be to God, who gives us the victory through our Lord Jesus Christ" (I Cor. 15:57). Death for the Christian becomes a transitional path from this life to the next; it is not a dead-end street but a thoroughfare that leads into another dimension of living. "Death is no more the dark door that shuts forever behind man," Brunner says, "but the opened door through which he enters into true life."[25]

Imagine how a baby might try to philosophize if he or she were able to contemplate another kind of life outside his or her mother's womb. What could she use as a base from which to speculate or surmise? How could she understand life free from surrounding liquid? What does she know of light, or breath, or food, or eating? What does he know of choices, companionship, friends, work, art, or reading? Is it not possible that to the infant the birth process is a crisis which is a sort of "death" as he or she leaves the safe, comfortable, secure world where every need had been met? A new and marvelous world awaits; he or she has no resources to imagine what it will be like and how wonderfully different from the other world. Death for the Christian is a "birthing" from the physical world to the spiritual realm. How can we possibly describe it; words fail us. "What no eye has seen, nor ear heard, nor the heart of man conceived, what God has prepared for those who love him" (1 Cor. 2:9).

The bandages were slowly being cut away from the eyes of the ten-year-old boy. He had been blind since birth. His parents waited, breathlessly hoping that he would now be able to see. The surgeon turned the boy's head toward the window and asked him to open his eyes slowly. At first the light was blinding but then his eyes began to focus on some flowers outside the window and the young lad shouted: "But why didn't you tell me it was so beautiful?" His father's only reply was, "We tried to, Son! We tried to."

When we open our eyes after the "birthing" from the physical to the spiritual realm and catch our first glimpses of the beauty and wonder of eternity, will we not also ask, "But why didn't you tell me it was so beautiful?" Our Lord will say, "I tried to!"

2

THE LAST JUDGMENT: HOW GOD SIZES US UP

When I was a boy, I recall going to my grandmother's house. She had a picture on the wall of a "Seeing Eye" that appeared to be looking at you. No matter where I went in the room this eye was looking at me. Below the eye there were people who seemed to be in a state of terror. The picture revealed the great eye of God that observed every single thing we said and did. I still can remember that eye looking at me today. It always left me a bit uneasy.

In the Sistine Chapel, Michelangelo depicted the Last Judgment in a powerful mural. In this mural he shows the goats on one side and the sheep on the other. The persons standing on the right, who have been received by Christ, have a look of surprise on their faces and remorse at what they see happening to those who have rejected Christ. Those on the left have terror on their faces as they are being pulled down by demons into the fiery pit of hell. Some of you may remember sermons you heard from evangelists and preachers who challenge you to prepare for the Day of Judgment. Jonathan Edwards' sermon, "Sinners in the Hands of An Angry God," depicts the great White Throne of God and all persons standing before it while a God of great anger and vindictiveness renders havoc upon all those who did not respond to Him. It is a frightening scene.

Today, in our modern world, I don't see, hear or sense many people who seem to be frightened about a day of judgment. Just look at the way many people act and live. Do you see many people today terrified that somehow or another the great judgment of

God is going to come upon them and God will do something to punish them? I don't think many people today have a great fear of Judgment Day.

Judgment is Real

But, I believe without question that the judgment of God is real. Whether modern society wants to accept it or not, the judgment of God is real. How can it not be? Several years ago I saw on a news program a serial killer who had killed and tortured a number of women. He had killed someone just to get a VCR. Is there no judgment for this kind of action? What do you say about a man like Hitler who had six million Jews put to death? There are those, in our own time, who have reeked havoc and death in Kosovo and in other places. What about child abusers or drug dealers who hurt others to support their habits? Is there no judgment?

If there is no judgment, does God not have any ethics? Our God is an ethical God. I believe that judgment is real and God doesn't just wink at what we do. Look at your sin and my sin. We all have committed sins. Too often our lives are filled with greed, selfishness, pride, jealousy, envy, and other large or small sins. Every single one of us has some dark side or spot in his or her life.

Look at the Old Testament. In the Old Testament prophets were often announcing judgment of God upon humanity. The flood was God's judgment on the sinfulness of humanity. The tower of Babel tells us of God's judgment on the confusion of humanity. The Old Testament prophets came again and again to Israel and warned them of their sins and how they had turned away from God. God executes judgment among the nations (Psalm 110:16) and judges the world with righteousness (Psalm 9:8) and the peoples with equity (Psalm 96:10).

In the New Testament, note especially the parables of Jesus. Notice the many references to judgment in Jesus' teachings. Look at the parables about the dragnet, the wheat and the tares, the wedding feast and those who come with an improper garment to the wedding feast, the wicked vineyard tenants, the barren fig tree, the Pharisee and the tax collector, the rich man and Lazarus and the sheep and the goats. All of these are parables told by Jesus and they speak about God's judgment.

Paul reminds us that every single person will stand before the judgment seat of God and give account of his or her deeds (Romans 14:10-12). The book of Revelation reminds us of the great white throne where men and women will be judged (Revelation 20:11-15). In symbolic images of the universal judgment of humanity both the living and the resurrected dead are portrayed.[1]

As We Enter God's Presence, We Are Judged

I believe that once we come into God's presence, judgment happens. How can you and I not feel judged when we come into God's presence and face the One who is wholly Other and we realize that we are sinners? We are already judged.

The Fourth Gospel states that Jesus came not into the world to condemn or judge the world but to bring light and to save it. "This is judgment that light has come" (John 3:19). Jesus is the "light of the world" (John 8:12). When we come into the light of the presence of Jesus, we see ourselves as we really are. When we remain in darkness, we are either unaware or unconcerned about our sins. They make no difference. Then, suddenly, in the focus of the light of the presence of Jesus, we see ourselves differently. The light makes all of the difference.

I can walk into my study without turning on the light on a dark night and it may not look so bad. But when I flip on the light switch, because I have been unusually busy recently, I have books piled high, my desk is covered with stacks of many things I haven't gotten around to. In some places books are stacked on top of books. The light reveals the clutter. The light makes it clear that everything is not neat and clean. My trash can needs emptying and many other things need to be addressed. How do I know this? Light comes and exposes things as they are. The darkness may conceal it, but the light makes it clear. When we come into the light of Jesus Christ, we see ourselves as we are—sinners.

Judgment Is a Present Reality

I believe that Judgment Day is both present and future. I think Judgment Day is not just something that happens in the future. Judgment has already begun today. We are judged hour by hour, day by day, week by week, and year by year. I am judged on the basis of what I do with the life I have been given. Every day our thoughts, words and deeds affect our lives. Everything we do affects our relationships to other people. What we put into the stream of life cannot be taken back. Once we commit something into the stream of life by an action, word or activity, it is then a part of who we are. Sometimes it affects others for good or for ill. Our souls are dyed the color of our thoughts and actions every single day. We are building the bridge of our lives plank by plank every day that we live. It is a continuous process and we are continuously being judged.

We Judge Ourselves in His Light

An interesting thing is that when we come into the light of Jesus Christ and he begins to cast his light upon us, we begin to judge ourselves. We are judged by that light. We then become self-judging. When we stand in the light of our Lord's presence, we see ourselves as we are and we judge ourselves in that light.

A man was going through a world famous art gallery. As he was leaving, he turned to the attendant and said, "I don't think much of these paintings." The attendant responded to him, "Sir, these pictures are not on trial." Christ is not on trial. His life, his standard, his values are not on trial, we are. We are judged by them. Our inadequacies, our flaws, our sins and our weaknesses are exposed.

Future Judgment

There is a future judgment, I believe. There is no question that judgment will take place sometime in the future. Jesus Christ is the standard and our lives are judged by Him. Although Jesus said that he came not to judge but to save, paradoxically, he still judges, nevertheless. He judges because we judge ourselves in the light of his revelation. Jesus said, "If any one hears my sayings and does not keep them, I do not judge him; for I did not come to judge the world but to save the world. He who rejects me and does not receive my sayings has a judge; the word that I have spoken will be his judge on the last day" (John 12:47-48).

When Does Judgment Happen?

When will this judgment come? Oh, you hear all kinds of projections from preachers and theologians. They often pick out selected parts of the Scriptures, especially from the symbolic book of Revelation, and then try to envision the kinds of things that are going to happen a thousand years or more down the road. Nobody knows! It has been two thousand years since Christ came and many of these theological witch doctors and so-called prophets want to tell us when Christ is coming and when he will judge the world. Jesus says nobody knows, except the Father! (Matthew 24:36)

We Are Judged At Our Own Death

Let me tell you when I think judgment will happen in the future. I believe that the judgment of God happens to every single individual when he or she dies and goes to be with God. I think that the day of the great white throne and all of the nations standing gathered before God happens instantaneously as we die and go to be with God in the spiritual realm.

I don't know a simple way to explain all of these mysterious things. Jesus told the thief on the cross, "Today you will be with me in paradise" (Luke 23:43). Jesus said, in response to the question of the Sadducees about marriage in heaven, "He is not the God of the dead but of the living" (Matthew 22:31-32). "I am the God of Abraham, Isaac, and the God of Jacob." What was Jesus saying? He was saying that the dead are still "living." There is just a step between this life and the next life and we go into God's presence then. I believe that when we step into God's presence that is when the judgment for you and me happens. It is not in a thousand years and not when we rise out of the grave. I believe that we rise immediately to be judged. We step from the physical world into the spiritual one. Time is not the same with God as with us.

How Are We Judged?

How shall we be judged? I think we are judged in our response to the highest revelation of God that we have had. You and I have heard the word of Jesus Christ and God expects us to respond to that word and commit our lives to that revelation. Many people seem to be worried about the heathen. They've never heard of Jesus; what will happen to them? Have they responded to the highest revelation they have? This is what Paul is writing about in Romans when he states that "what can be known about God is plain to them, because God has shown it to them" (Romans 1:19. See also Romans 2 and 3).

They have seen God through creation and their inner conscience. Have they responded to the highest revelation that has come to them? If so, they have responded to the eternal Christ, who works in all kinds of ways and maybe even through all kinds of religions to tell us about the reality of God's grace and presence. I believe that when we die, we begin with God wherever we leave off in this world. That relationship may not be exactly the same for every one of us.

Our Response to Others Is Crucial

I think we need to remember that when we talk about Christ as the highest revelation, this is also a call to us to remember how we respond to other people as well. No one loves Jesus Christ in isolation. We love Christ in relationship to other people. "Inasmuch as you have done it to the least of these, you have done it unto me," Jesus said (Matt. 25:40).

Edward Irving was pastor in a London church. He had engraved on the silver offering trays in his church that if the church ever got to the point that the offerings which they took up were not sufficient to take care of the needs of the poor, that the sacred vessels were to be melted down to supply the deficiency. What is this telling us? We serve Christ by helping others in society, not hoarding life to ourselves.

Grace Is Greater Than Law

When we stand before the Judgment Seat of God, we will experience grace, thank goodness, and not just law. It is easy to put fear in the hearts of people, if we are always concerned about legalism when we stand before God. The Scriptures tell us that God so loved the world that He gave His Son. Grace is greater than the law. R. Kirby Godsey has affirmed this truth with these words, "Judgment comes for the sake of redemption."[2] God is not interested in "getting even" with us but in loving us back to goodness and righteousness.

I don't know how you picture your Day of Judgment. In my eye, I picture that, when I die and stand before the Lord, the Lord isn't going to say anything to me. I don't believe that the Lord is going to stand there and talk to me. As I find myself before the Lord, the first thing I am going to do is drop to my knees. In the light of Jesus Christ and all his glory, I am going to know suddenly all of my inadequacies. I am going to know where I have fallen short and sinned. He is not going to have to tell me. Simply being in his presence is going to reveal that to me.

When I know my needs, I am going to seek to go into God's kingdom to the level where I can continue to grow and develop deeper in my relationship to Christ. Some are on a higher plain spiritually than others. Some are so low spiritually that for them, this is Hell. They are far from God. There are others, even Christians, saved by grace, who will be spiritually on different plateaus. We are not going to know where anybody else is. It's like each one of us has a spiritual cup. I know how much is in my cup, but I don't know how much spiritual life is in your cup. Frankly, I know that is not my concern, unless I am a teacher who is going to help others move further along the spiritual plain. I don't think that when we arrive in the heavenly realm that we are full-grown Christians.

I think we will have eternity to keep growing and seeking to be more like God.

Jürgen Moltmann has projected the Last Judgment not as a time to be dreaded but as an occasion for restoration.

> 'The Last Judgment' is not a terror. In the truth of Christ it is the most wonderful thing that can be proclaimed to men and women. It is a source of endlessly consoling joy to know, not just that the murderers will finally fail to triumph over their victims, but that they cannot in eternity even remain the murderers of their victims. The eschatological doctrine about the restoration of all things has these two sides: *God's Judgment, which puts things to rights, and God's kingdom, which awakens to new life.*[3]

A young man came to his pastor and said, "Pastor, how can I find the peace of God in my life." The pastor said, "I'm sorry you're too late." "Too late to be saved?" the lad asked. "Oh, no," said the pastor, "It's not that. It's too late for you to try to create peace with God. Because it's already been done." Jesus Christ did it. He created that avenue of peace centuries ago, once and for all. Now we have to respond to it. God has already given us grace, let's respond to it. When we do, we will experience that God's judgment is good.

Surprises in Judgment

I believe there will be some great surprises in God's judgment. When we read the passage from the 25th chapter of Matthew, the interesting thing from our Lord's lips is that there is no indication that we are redeemed by our theology, our doctrines, our church attendance or any of these things. This is not the way we relate to Him. Profession without practice is meaningless. Those who put so much emphasis on right thinking, right theology, dotting the theological line, and being more orthodox than others, are going to be greatly surprised when they stand before the judgment of God.

Our Response to Human Need

In this passage Jesus tells us we are judged and sized up by how we respond to human need around us. Whether you have helped people in the smallest kinds of things, such as in illness, hunger, prison, sickness or whatever, that is meeting human need. As we respond to human need, this response is done naturally and instinctively. We cannot say, "Well let's see what I can do to gain favor in God's kingdom." You don't get God's approval that way. Note that these people did not even know they were doing anything for Jesus. They were surprised, unaware that they had done anything for him. They simply saw a need and responded.

Examine Ourselves

I don't know about you but I sometimes become very uncomfortable with the New Testament. I know what I want to think it says, but when I read it, it forces me to look at myself under the microscope of God's grace and God's judgment. As God's judgment comes into my life, it begins to say to me that the most important things in my life are not my possessions, fame, wealth or prestige. The most important fact is whether or not I have done something to care for others in times of need. I don't know about you but I find that I measure up very short by that.

As much work as I do in the church, I still feel that I fall very short by God's standard. Compared to Mother Teresa, who gave up everything, her every possession, to care for the dying in India, who in the world am I? What in the world have I ever done compared to Albert Schweitzer who gave up everything to go to Africa to serve Christ? How far short I fall compared to some friends I know who are working in Hell's Kitchen in New York City with young people on drugs and seeking to find themselves! I don't know how you think you measure up, but when it comes to the judgment of Christ, I know that I have a long way to grow in emptying myself of self-centeredness, my hunger for things, and in seeking to serve the Lord.

We Minister to Christ Through Others

One of the interesting things in this picture of the Last Judgment is that Jesus tells us that when we help other people in times of need, we are serving him and ministering to him. We may not even know it. The persons who served Jesus, whom he praised, probably had none of the so-called right theology. That is one of the surprises of this passage. Jesus said in another place, "you will know my disciples by their fruits" (Matthew 7:16). James stated, "Faith without works is dead" (James 2:17). How does God size us up? Is it by whether or not we have correct theology or whether or not we are reaching out to serve others in his kingdom?

Martin of Tours one day met a beggar on the road, who was shivering and cold. Martin took his outer garment and cut it in half and gave half of his soldier's coat to him so that he could wrap himself up and keep warm. That night Martin had a dream. In his dream he saw Jesus and he was wearing half of Martin's coat around him. Some of the angels were asking Jesus, "Why are you wearing that dirty old coat?" Jesus said, "I was cold and my servant Martin cut his coat in half and shared it with me." Inasmuch as you do it unto the least of these my brethren, you have done it unto me. Christian service is "the utmost for the lowest."

Surprisingly Condemned

Hear this word. There are those on one side of the throne who are the sheep who get the word from Jesus, "well done." But there are those who are condemned and even they did not know. "Lord, when did we NOT do something for you?" That is one of the surprises. Not choosing to do anything is choosing.

As you choose in life, realize what is most valuable. Shouldn't the most valuable thing be to find ways that we can serve Christ to get beyond our selfishness and materialism so that we can hear him say, "well done"? The way God sizes us up is surprisingly different from the way we often think.

3

THE SECOND COMING: CHRIST CAME AND COMES

I can remember as a teenager, hearing many stories and interpretations about The Second Coming of Jesus. These stories always focused on Jesus returning suddenly and unexpectedly. A man's car collides with another car because he is snatched from his car and taken to be with Jesus. A plane crashes, killing everyone on board because the pilot is taken up with Jesus. One man is lifted from his fishing boat, another is left. A husband is left standing in his kitchen because his wife is gone. All of these departures come with a sense of suddenness and terror fills the world. God seems to be angry, vindictive, and vengeful.

The same kind of philosophy is depicted today in the fiction of writers like Tim LaHaye and Jerry Jenkins' book, *Left Behind.*[1] Some of these writers have projected that the year 2000 was going to mark the time of the Second Coming of Christ. Jerry Falwell said it would be within ten years after 2000. All of these literal interpretations are based on a few verses of Scripture and, in my opinion, a radical misunderstanding of what the coming of Christ is. Some have made predictions and promises of perilous times before the tribulation and chronicle a long list of catastrophic coming events before the rapture.[2]

No Clear System on the Second Coming in the Bible

Let me begin by saying the New Testament teachings cannot be put into any one clear system. Many have tried to do this. You read the Scriptures and there is no question that passage after passage speaks of the coming one. Luke 21:27 says, "And they will see the son of man coming in a cloud with power and great glory." In John 14:2, Jesus said, "I have gone to prepare a place for you and after that I will come again and receive you unto myself." In Acts 1:11, we read, "this Jesus who was taken up from you into heaven will come in the same way as you saw him go into heaven."

Paul in almost all of his writings, except maybe Galatians, Ephesians and Philemon, speaks about the coming of Christ. At first Paul wrote in a sense of expecting an immediate return. Later he begins to change his view. Even as we observe the Lord's Supper, Paul has reminded us that "we do this until the Lord comes," (1 Corinthians 11:26). James suggested the coming of Christ was near at hand" (James 5:8). Revelation is filled with all kinds of apocalyptic symbols, especially in Chapters 19, 20 and 21.

A Variety of Interpretations

Jesus Was Mistaken

What sense are we to make of all of these verses, including the ones in Matthew 16:28 and 24:3-36? Let's begin by saying that there have been many different interpretations about the Second Coming. One writer, for example, said that Jesus was mistaken in his own views of the end of the ages. Jesus went to the cross to force God to bring in the kingdom of God. When he was dying on the cross, Jesus realized he was mistaken, and that is why he cried, "My God, My God, why have you forsaken me?" Albert Schweitzer set forth this view.[3] He didn't have many scholars that agreed with him, but it was his interpretation.

Postmillennialist

Another popular position is called the postmillennialist view. These advocates believe that a sign that the end is near is realized in the return of Israel to the Holy Land. They believe that the world is improving and that Christ will remain in heaven and work through his church to redeem the world. At the end of a thousand years Christ will come and intervene in the world and bring history to its conclusion.[4]

Premillennialist

You may be familiar with the premillennialist view. These persons take the opposite view of the postmillienialists, instead of the world getting better they believe that it is getting more evil. For them too, the return of Israel to its homeland was a sign of the end. The rapture is going to take the saints out of this world. After seven years of tribulation, there will be a thousand-year reign of Christ, and then the judgment will come. There are four resurrections and five judgments in this theory. It is very complicated. They have developed charts and graphs to help people understand their beliefs.

Amillennialist

There are some who hold to what is called the amillennialist view. To them the thousand-year reign is just symbolic. Christ began reigning on the cross, and he is continuing to reign and will reign until the end of history.

Someone has said that he was a panmillennialist. "It's all going to pan out in the end anyway so why worry about it." He may make more sense than some of the others who take a few isolated verses and build their theological systems around them. There are only three verses in Revelation that these individuals have built unbelievably complicated systems upon. In fact you have to understand their whole interpretation of the Bible to agree to their interpretation. I think Kirby Godsey is on target when he states that "chasing after a literal rendering of these passages and transcribing them into the complicated theories of the millennium is a mistake."[5]

Only One Coming

Some believe that dividing the eschatological event of the coming of Christ into two comings is to be traced to the church and not to Jesus. John A. T. Robinson, an English Bishop, writes, "There is but one coming, begun at Christmas, perfected on the cross, and continuing until all are included in it."[6]

Pentecost

There are others who believe that the Second Coming was realized at Pentecost. At Pentecost, these advocates believe that Jesus came in the form of the Holy Spirit. He came with power and, with the pouring out of his spirit, he kept all his promises in which he said he would come again. These positions are just a few of the many interpretations New Testament scholars and theologians have given about the Second Coming.

Some Important Considerations

Not in the New Testament

In trying to understand the concept of the Second Coming, I think we need to be aware of a few things. You need to be aware that the words, "Second Coming," do not appear in the New Testament. The closest you can find anywhere is in Hebrews 9:28, "He shall appear a second time, apart from sin, to those awaiting him unto salvation." The earliest use of the term comes about the middle of the second century. The New Testament term in Greek is "Parousia" which means "presence" or "coming."

Consistent with the Character of Jesus

I think, when we try to understand any view of Christ's coming, we have got to make it consistent with the character of Jesus.

The revelation of God which we have seen in Jesus needs to continue to be consistent with any interpretation we give of Jesus in any future coming. In the book of Revelation, some draw on an image of a warrior Messiah who is going to overcome the world with force and terror. This "warring Messiah" is not consistent with the Gospel's picture of Jesus. Jesus never used force or vengeance. Jesus told Peter to put up the sword. Jesus sought to draw people to him out of love. He turned the other cheek and went the second mile.

There is no way that one can speak of Jesus as being vengeful when he even forgave those who crucified him as he was dying on the cross. Jesus rejected all physical force in seeking to bring in his kingdom. In fact, Revelation states that it is the blood of the Lamb that overcomes the world (Revelation 1:5f). The victory was realized in the death and resurrection of Jesus who reigns forever and ever (Revelation 11:15).

Type of Literature and World view

You also have to consider the type of biblical literature and world view that was held in biblical times. Much of the literature about the Second Coming is called "apocalyptic." Daniel and Revelation are good examples of this literature. "Apocalyptic" means unveiling or revealing. This literature is not meant to be taken literally. Matthew 24:4-21 is called the "Little Apocalypse." Mark 13:5-37 and Luke 17:22-37 contain similar images. The basic theme is judgment and separation of good and evil.

Too many people try to take the Book of Revelation and read it literally. It is a drama. Its teachings were directed to Christian people suffering persecution under the Roman government, probably Emperor Domitian. The book was written not primarily as a projection into the far-off yonder about God. It was trying to help first century Christians understand how they were to live under the vindictiveness and the forcefulness of a government that was persecuting them. This book sought to give them courage and sustained them during a time of persecution, suffering and martyrdom. The numbers, images, or figures in Revelation are not to be taken literally. Unfortunately, many try to do so.

The Delay of Jesus' Coming

What do we say about the delay of Jesus' coming? "This generation will not pass away until all these things be accomplished" (Mark 13:30; Matthew 24:34)—"This generation." "Some of those standing here who will not taste of death before they have seen the kingdom of God come in power" (Mark 9:1). This expectation of an imminent return and the assurance that some of them would live to see his "parousia" or coming are the reasons some have seen his "coming" at Pentecost in the Holy Spirit. Any implication that the end was near needs to be understood in the reminder from Jesus: "No one knows the day or the hour, only the Father" (Matthew 24:36). All of this should help us to see how complicated it is to try to understand what is meant by the "Second Coming."

How Are We to Understand the "Parousia" or Coming of Jesus?

Affirm Jesus' Presence Today

How do we understand this concept of parousia or the Second Coming? Let me state first that I do not believe that we can speak of a future coming in a way that denies the presence of Christ today. We do not follow an absent Lord. Our Lord is not away some place, apart from us. Jesus said, "Lo, I am with you always" (Matthew 28:20). "I have come that you might have life and have it more abundantly" (John 10:10). "I stand at the door and knock, and if anyone will open, I will come in and sup with him" (Revelation 3:20). "For me to live is Christ," (Philippians 1:20), Paul says. "The word became flesh and dwelt among us" (John 1:14)—the Incarnation. "You abide in me," Jesus said, "and I in you" (John 15:4). John 14 reminds us that Jesus "will come again and receive us unto himself" (John 14:3).

In our churches we call people to come and make a commitment to Jesus Christ as a living Lord, not as an absent Lord. We ask them to open their hearts that Jesus might come in and bring them redemption today. Jesus said, "I am the resurrection and the life" (John 11:25). He is not someone absent, but is present! We affirm that there is the power of Christ's presence with us through the Holy Spirit today. Whatever we say about a future coming of Jesus cannot be a denial of the reality of Jesus among us today.

At Death We Experience Our Lord's Coming

Secondly, at our death, I believe that we experience our personal encounter of the Second Coming of Christ. At the moment of the believer's death, we encounter the Lord on his throne in the clouds of glory, high and lifted up. As we meet the Lord, we feel judged in the light of his coming in his full glory.

Remember that God's awareness of time is totally different from ours. The Scriptures say a thousand years are as a day to God. God is not trapped in time like we are. All of our concepts of the millennium, the rapture, the resurrection and judgment are caught up in the present reign of Christ. I do not think there is any delay. I think we are resurrected immediately into the presence of Christ and our future is moved into immediacy. At our death, we encounter the "coming" of Christ, his "Second Coming" into our lives.

History Has Meaning

Third, whatever the future dimension of the Second Coming is, it assures us that history is going somewhere. History will not end in chaos or aimlessness, meaninglessness or futility. The cosmos and humanity, as Paul writes about it in Romans (Romans 8:22ff), is moving toward the ultimate redemption by God. We all need complete redemption. None of us is fully redeemed. The figures or redemption in the New Testament are depicted as "new births" not "new ends." Redemption is a new beginning. Yeast and mustard seeds are signs of growth. As one commits his or her life to Christ, no one is a completely full-grown Christian instantly. We are in the life-time process of growing toward being like Christ. We have an eternity to continue to grow to be like our Lord.

The coming of Jesus in the clouds image is an "ascent," a sign of the reign of Christ among us. Will this reign be on earth or in heaven? I don't know. Whatever this reign is, I think it is a spiritual reign. The Book of Revelation tells us that God is going to be in charge of things. I do not believe that we can ever fully know God's presence. We are always in the process of becoming. Whatever the meaning of the images of the "coming" of Jesus are, I believe the basic purpose is to show us the power and the reign of God (Matthew 24:30). The image of "lightening" in Matthew 24:27 is a sign of the universal significance of the reign of Christ. All persons at some point will be under the rule and power of the living Lord. Moltmann believes that the emphasis on a historical millenarianism or "last Big Bang" is catastrophic, while Christian eschatology is "messianic, healing and saving."[7]

"How Are We To Live?"

Be Watchful

What are we to do as we think and prepare for the Second Coming? The Scriptures tell, I believe, that we have received a call to be alert, watchful and faithful in our Christian walk. The Scriptures warn us against false prophets. Anyone who tells you that the Second Coming is in ten years from now, or a thousand years, or next week, don't pay them any attention. Jesus says, "No one knows!" I don't care who the preacher or theologian is. No one knows for sure but God!

Worldwide Problems

We are also told in Matthew that there are going to be all kinds of secular catastrophes, terrors and evils in the world. Every time some catastrophic thing happens or evil is done, people jump to the assumption that the world is coming to an end. But people have been saying that for centuries, ever since the time of Jesus. Terrors, evil and natural calamities are a part of the world in which we live.

Universal Proclamation

This passage in Matthew assures us that Jesus is not coming until the message of God's salvation has been proclaimed around the whole world. Many of us forget that verse. There are a lot of dark corners, even in our own neighborhoods, where the Gospel hasn't been preached yet. I don't think we are anywhere close to the final end of history. No one knows when Jesus' coming is. What we are called to do is to live in trust. "He that endureth to the end will be saved," (Matthew 24:13). There will be all kinds of persecutions and pressures upon us to turn away from the faith. "Be faithful unto death," (Rev.2:10). Live in trust, looking for the reign of Christ in the world. "The message of the millennium," N.T. Wright affirms, "should be that the principalities and powers that still tyrannize this sorry old world are not in fact its rightful lord, and that Jesus is."[8]

The Reign of Christ

What is the trumpet that Matthew mentions (Matthew 24:31)? This trumpet is the note of God's victory. Christ is reigning in the hearts and lives of people. Three times in Revelation, Jesus is spoken of as the Alpha and the Omega, the beginning and the end (Revelation 1:8, 21:6, 22:13). What is its significance? In Jesus Christ, everything has its beginning and completeness in him. He is the beginning and the end of all things.

Several years ago there was a book entitled, *What To Do Until the Messiah Comes.* I'll tell you what I think we ought to do. Be faithful, be watchful. Let none of us be arrogant as though he or she knows all about God's coming, God's grace and how God reigns. We need to be alert and open to wherever God's presence can come into our lives.

I believe that when one individual comes to Jesus Christ, he or she opens his or her life to Christ and Jesus comes into that life.

That is Jesus' coming to them. After that coming, we seek to follow Jesus. When we die and step into eternity, Jesus comes into our lives in a new way. He brings judgment, yes, but there is judgment with love, grace and his presence. I think our responsibility is to be ready. Be prepared!

A man came to see his pastor one day. He had just gone to see his doctor and his doctor had told him that he had cancer and less than a year to live. "Pastor," the man said, "I don't know what to do. I feel destitute. I am a very wealthy man. I could walk into any bank and borrow whatever sum of money I want on my name alone. But when it comes to facing an illness like this I know that I am spiritually destitute. There are some things you just can't borrow."

You can't borrow someone else's faith. You can't borrow someone else's sense of the presence of Jesus Christ in your life. That's the reason each person has to come to Christ. Each one has to open his or her life to Jesus Christ. If we commit our life to Christ today, then we can live our life in trust. I don't know about you, but I can trust him today, tomorrow and I can trust him in my dying.

4

HELL: VINDICTIVE OR REMEDIAL?

Let me begin by saying that in all of my years of ministry there has probably been no topic over which I have struggled and agonized as much as this one. I am not someone who takes delight in preaching or writing about hell. I share with you now my gleanings and understandings from the Scriptures of what I think is a proper perspective on hell.

Most of us today, if we have any image of hell at all, have one that is usually drawn from some horror movies we have seen or some version of Dante's Inferno. In Dante's Inferno, Dante is conducted through the realm of damnation where souls of men and women receive eternal punishment that is appropriate to the kinds of sins they have committed. The journey follows nine levels of hell which descend downward in a cone-like shape, deeper and deeper into the earth until it finally reaches the region of the worst sinners who are frozen in ice. The three-headed Lucifer is at the center of the earth.

Years ago, people were often terrified by fundamentalist preachers and evangelists who preached hell-fire and damnation sermons. These preachers today or their stereotypes receive only jeers, laughter, ridicule, polite hearings or they are simply ignored. Most do not listen, heed or take seriously such sermons today. People are largely indifferent to these sermons and when or if they hear them, they yawn or sleep through them.[1] An article carried by the Associated Press, written by Richard N. Ostling (Richmond Times Dispatch, June 16, 2006}, notes that there has been a declining belief in heaven and hell in recent years. "Some people suppose that hell must be conceived as a non-place," Piero Camporesi notes, "while others speak of it unwillingly, somewhat embarrassed, as a worn-out metaphor."[2]

Others almost seem to rejoice or take pleasure in knowing that someone else may be going to hell. I have heard preachers speak in such a way to their congregations that they almost seem to be delighted to tell their listeners that they were going to hell. Others have feared hell for themselves but have wished it or cursed it on others.

When we read the New Testament, we discover that, although Jesus had great compassion for sinners, he used some of his harshest language for God's judgment upon sin. Jesus spoke of the shut door (Matthew 25:10), outer darkness (Matthew 8:12), and unquenchable fire (Mark 9:48). He spoke about weeping and gnashing of teeth (Matthew 25:30), the furnace of fire (Matthew 13:42) and the fire and worm (Mark 9:48). He spoke of a son who was lost and dead (Luke 15:24).

Many sensitive and committed Christians today do not know what to make of such horrible words from the one who came to seek and to save the lost. How do we understand such an awful teaching in the light of a God of love, grace and mercy and from one who taught us to forgive, seventy times seven or endlessly (Matthew 18:22)?

Hell Does Exist

So, let me begin by saying, first of all, I believe that hell does exist. I believe that hell is real. "Hell," as Emil Brunner, the Swiss Theologian said, "is unconditional, irrevocable, godforsakenness and unconditional despair."[3] Hell is the barrier between God and a hardened heart. Hell begins in this life as one rejects God, the way of Christ, is unrepentant and focuses primarily upon one's own selfishness. As Nels F. S. Ferré writes, "Hell is not heaven unattained but heaven rejected. Hell is both the condition and consequence of the unrepentant life."[4] In a lighter vain Henlee Barnette, former professor of ethics at the Southern Baptist Theological Seminary in Louisville, Kentucky, told one time about his response to some accusations that the seminary faculty wasn't orthodox enough, Barnette gave the following response to his assigned topic, "Why I Believe in Hell." He said that he believed in hell for three reasons: "1. Jesus taught it; 2. People who give it to other people ought to get some of their own; 3. I've been there."

A Consequence of Decisions Made In This Life

Hell is the consequence of a sin-filled life. Our character is formed by what we say and by what we do. As we give way to sin, our lives are shaped by it and, as time gathers momentum, we make choices, decisions, deeds, and actions that become habits. They mold us into who and what we are. We may have chosen a path that leads to evil actions and its consequences. We may have closed the door to God, to goodness, to the Christ-like way or sometimes even to plain decency. Sin has become a way of life for us. We, frankly, are uncomfortable around religion, the church or godly ways. We have chosen to cut ourselves off and to be separated from God.

This choice was ours, not God's. Our fate depends upon our choice and our conduct. Some may get to the point that they no longer respond to goodness or righteousness at all. How else can we explain someone like Hitler, mass murderers, terrorists, child abusers, or dictators who kill anybody who gets in their way, sometimes whole villages or towns?

God Gives Us Freedom

Remember, God has created us with freedom. God will not force or coerce anyone into loving Him. We are free to follow God's way or not. Surely no one can say that a person is free to reject God's way, laugh at God's moral and spiritual laws, mock the Christian way, ridicule Christ and the church, continue to follow a sinful way and still be within God's will. Suppose a person chooses to turn away from God and will not be converted. Where is that individual in eternity with God?

C. S. Lewis has reminded us that there is a difference between condoning and forgiving.

> To condone an evil is simply to ignore, to treat it as if it were good. But forgiveness needs to be accepted as well as offered if it is to be complete: and a man [or woman] who admits no guilt can accept no forgiveness.[5]

Again he writes,

> In the long run, the answer to those who object to the doctrine of hell is itself a question: 'What are you asking God to do?' To wipe out the past sins and, at all costs give them a fresh start, smoothing every difficulty and offering every miraculous help? But He has done so on Calvary. To forgive them? They will not be forgiven. He will leave them alone? Alas, I am afraid that is what He does.[6]

The Scriptures remind us that it is possible to lose one's relationship with God. Paul reminds us in Galatians that God is not to be trifled with. We will reap what we sow (Galatians 6:8). Jesus said there is a path that leads to life and there is a path that leads to destruction (Matthew 7:13). Each person chooses. Hell is the state of those who have decided not to know God.

The Public Incinerator

Hell comes from a Greek word, *Gehenna,* which referred to the garbage dump or the public incinerator outside the gates of Jerusalem. The fires burned constantly as it consumed the rubbish of the city. The image was a vivid, familiar one to the people in the day of Jesus.

Various Interpretations of Hell

Again, there is no one correct interpretation of Hell as you read the Scriptures. Many theologians and New Testament scholars have drawn on various theories to try to understand it. Let me offer you a few of these before I give you my basic thoughts.

Ancient Mythology

Some have said that hell is simply ancient mythology. It should be discarded in our modern world. We are too mature for that image they say. We should move beyond it and not focus on tales that frighten and seek to control us.

I don't know if you saw the cartoon where Peppermint Patty and Marcie are talking in one of the *Peanuts* comic strips. They are standing in a religious camp and Peppermint Patty is saying to the director, "Yes, Ma'am, I'd like to use the telephone . . . my Dad hasn't heard about the end of the world." "Look at this, Sir," Marcie says as she points to something on the wall. "There's a drawing of the new camp they're trying to raise money for. It should be very beautiful. They are asking everyone to help raise eight million dollars!" Peppermint Patty turns around to the director and says, "Forget the phone, Ma'am! Maybe the world will end tomorrow, but I wasn't born yesterday."[7]

Do you hear what she is saying? There are some who use hell and other religious means as scare tactics just to raise money for themselves.

A Literal Hell

Others take hell literally and believe it is the punishment of the unregenerate, who are excluded from the blessings of Heaven and are in torment. These advocates believe that the wicked are getting retributive justice and judgment for their sins. They see this punishment, not as vindictive, but as justice for breaking God's spiritual and moral laws.

Annihilation

There are others who believe that after death, annihilation takes place. They believe we are either extinguished at death or at some point beyond in the final judgment. Believers in this view draw on Scriptures such as, "Whoever wishes to save his life shall destroy it" (Mark 8:35). "Who shall suffer punishment, even eternal destruction from the face of the Lord and from the glory of his might?" (2 Thessalonians 1:9). "The heavens and earth that now exist have been stored up with fire, being kept until the day of judgment and destruction upon godly men" (2 Peter 3:7). "Death and Hell are thrown into the lake of fire" (Revelation 20:14). People draw upon such words as death, destruction, abolishing, perishing, and perdition. According to this theory, nothing continues after death. This belief seems to me to be at odds with most of the teachings of Jesus, Paul and other New Testament writers.

A Place of Restoration

There are others who feel that hell is a place of restoration. This view advocates that those who are not in harmony with God in this life will experience in hell a time of teaching, preparation, and testing to enable them to find fellowship with God in the blessed life later. Some believe that the punishment and suffering will change the mind and character of those who have rejected God. They will turn to God in the present or sometime in the future.

Others contend that if punishment and suffering are not enough, God will use more powerful mean of persuasion. Others hold to the viewpoint that at some point or another Jesus will preach to them and they will be given an opportunity to repent.

What View Can We Hold Today?

Eternal

How are we to perceive of hell today? Let's begin by looking at the Greek word, "Eternal." What is the meaning of the word that translates, "Eternal Punishment." The Greek word, "eternal," does not mean "endless." It means "belonging to a coming age." In Hebrew it means "for a long time," and in Greek, "age upon age." It does not refer to a duration of time. It isn't a reference to timelessness. It means "age-long." Our word "*aeon*" is derived from it.

Time is not a word that has meaning in the spiritual realm. Because we live in time, we cannot imagine something not being judged by time. We judge everything by seconds, minutes, hours, days, weeks, months, years, and centuries. In the scriptures, "time" in the "eternal life" is not relevant. The reference likely refers to a state or condition- punishment or separation or one who is in a state of growing in some spiritual blessedness. We are always in the process of growing closer to God.

Remedial

Is it possible that hell may be remedial? Could this period of time, whatever it is, be an opportunity for growth for the people who are there? If one begins in the next life where he or she leaves off here, is it possible that individual may be far from God and need "age upon age"-a duration of time, "eon after eon" to respond to God's love? Is there a possibility of change? Does punishment have any meaning other than vindictiveness, if it does not offer an opportunity for change and reformation in character? What is its purpose? If punishment is endless, what is its value?

If a person never has a chance to change if he or she wants to, does that mean that God is really omnipotent, all powerful? Has the wideness, the length, the height, the breadth, and the depth of God's love been defeated if a person continues to reject it? I believe that Jonathan L. Kvanvig's observation is correct, "Any solution to the problem of hell will have to deal with the nature of God's goodness and the motivation he has for creating the possibilities of heaven and hell in the first place."[8]

If a parent is concerned about a lost child, can the Good Shepherd who would leave the ninety and nine to go out looking for the one lost sheep, be satisfied until this child ultimately responds to the father's love? No matter what a child has done, the parent would not keep on punishing that child for the rest of his or her life. If it is true of a parent, how much more is it true of God? Jesus said, "If you then, being evil, know how to give good gifts unto your children, how much shall your Father, which is in heaven, give good things to them that ask of him" (Luke 11:13).

What if the person chooses not to respond to God's love, but remains in isolation and despair? God grants that person that freedom. Is Nels Ferré possibly correct when he states that we must "preach hell as having a school and a door in it?"[9] Does that not mean that hell may be educational and remedial, a place where we can learn and still respond to God? Some feel that this is in keeping with the one who came "to seek and to save the lost" (Luke 9:10) and who proclaimed, "if I be lifted up, I will draw all persons to me" (John 12:32).

The Universal Power of Christ

The New Testament affirms the universal power of Christ over evil. It says of him, "every knee shall bow in heaven and on earth, and under the earth" (Romans 14:11). In I Peter 4:6 there is a striking image of Jesus. "For that is why the dead also had the gospel preached to them—that it might judge the lives they lived as men and give them also the opportunity to share the eternal life of God in the Spirit" (Moffat translation). In this passage, Christ is pictured as preaching to those in hell. Christ ascended into hell to deliver us from it. When the Apostle's Creed declares that Jesus descended into hell, is this a crack, window or glimpse into the realm of the dead? To whom does Jesus preach? Is it to those who rejected Noah, those who lived before Jesus came? Is it Adam and Eve? Is it Cain and Abel? Is it Judas? Is it those who haven't responded to the love of God? The Son seems to plant the cross in hell itself. Is this what the book of Revelation is saying when it speaks about the one who has the "keys of hell and death" in his hands (Revelation 1:18)? Was the promise of forgiveness to the thief on the cross also the promise of the forgiveness to others?

Molly Marshall, a theologian and president of Central Baptist Theological Seminary, examines 1 Peter 3:18-19 and 4:6 and discusses the difficulty of explaining the meaning of Jesus' "descended into hell" phrase. She interprets this to mean that even the realm of the dead cannot "hold prisoners when the resurrection power is loosed." No one, she notes, travels the path of suffering unaccompanied and death is not the final act. "Because faith comes by hearing, fides ex audio," she states, "the Gospel is preached even to those thought to be beyond the scope of Christ's redemption-the dead. The iconography of the church portrays a scene of liberation as forbears overcome corruptible death through Jesus."[10] Is the writer of 1 Peter trying to tell his readers that there is possibly a cosmic dimension in the reconciling death of Jesus Christ that opens God's grace even in Sheol? Is he urging us to consider the wideness of God's redeeming grace? In discussing 1 Peter 4:6 Dale Moody, former professor of theology at the Southern Baptist Theological Seminary, asks whether this passage suggests that the "righteous dead" are given a "first chance". "It is difficult indeed to believe that God would leave men forever in Hades simply because they never had a chance to hear the Gospel."[11]

The fifteenth century artist, Baldovinetti, has a painting in which he depicts the gates of hell as having been knocked off their hinges. Jesus is standing on the gates of hell, victorious, while the persons in hell are storming out and seeking to find freedom. This is called "the Harrowing of Hell."

George William Ruther has some pointed lines about Jesus' descent into hell and how he continues to harrow today.

> The mind can speculate about this because Christ did not end his "eternity save a day" in hell when he rose from the dead. Whenever the archaism of cynicism tries to suffocate the breath of grace, he harrows: he harrows every family table to compare what it is doing to the Heavenly Banquet, harrows every bedroom to compare it to Eden, and harrows every lecture to compare its declarations to the Sermon on the Mount."[12]

Jesus has come to bring us to God. He comes to redeem and reconcile us. Just as a father would go into a tavern to get a son overcome by drunkenness and bring him home. Doesn't God reach out to bring all persons unto him? Jesus says, "The hour is coming, and now is, when the dead shall hear the voice of the Son of God and they shall hear and live" (John 5:25, 11:43). In Ephesians 4, Paul says he ascended but he also descended into the lower parts of the earth . . . that he might fulfill all things" (Ephesians 4:9).

I know that no one can be so high in his or her spiritual life that he or she cannot still be drawn closer to God. Is it possible that no one can be so low that he or she cannot still be drawn to God? Walter Rauschenbusch, a noted Baptist theologian, believes that no Christian should rejoice in the idea of an eternal hell. He said that this doctrine could not be tolerable when one conceives of a Father dealing with his children. Punishment can no longer be viewed as wholly without end or change but needs to be seen as educational and redemptive.[13] He felt that something would die in heaven if God allowed a minority to remain in a permanent hell. If men and women choose to remain in darkness, Rauschenbusch asserted that there would be a Christian invasion of hell. He states further:

> All the most mature Christian souls in heaven would
> go down there and share the life of the wicked in the
> high hope, that after all some scintilla of heavenly fire
> was still smouldering and could be fanned into life. And
> they would be headed by Him who could not stand it
> to think of ninety-nine saved and one caught among the
> thorns.[14]

Christ Is Victor

However one may react to this view, we have to say that Christ is victorious over death and hell. "I am the first and the last, the living one, I died and behold I am alive forever more and I have the keys of death and hell" (Revelation 1:17). "Lo, I am with you always" (Matthew 28:20). The New Testament affirms Christ's reign and sovereignty. "Every knee shall bow and confess that Jesus Christ is Lord" (Philippians 2:10). "God has shut up all disobedience that he might have mercy upon them" (Romans 11:32).

Leave Judgment to God

I think we need to be very careful in categorizing those who are lost and those who are saved. Remember the picture of the final judgment in Matthew 25 with the sheep and the goats. Some responded to Jesus, "Lord, when did we do these things in your name and when did we not do these things?" It is so easy sometimes to pass judgment on others or to think that we are okay with God. The whole purpose of the story of the wheat and the tares in Matthew 13 is to remind us that we must leave judgment to God. God is the only one who has the right to judge—God and God alone.

The Power of God's Mercy

I believe in the power of God's mercy. I do not claim to know whether anyone ultimately can reject God's grace. I believe that God will grant a person that freedom. "However long an individual may reject his maker," John Hick writes, "salvation will remain an open possibility to which God is ever trying to draw him."[15] Whether that is true or not, I leave it in the hands of God. Moltmann, however, has expressed this view even stronger.

> Christ gave himself up for the lost in order to seek all who are lost, and to bring them home. He suffered the torments of hell, in order to throw hell open, so that these torments are no longer without hope of an end. Because he suffered hell, he gives hope where otherwise 'all hope must be abandoned', as Dante said. Because Christ was brought out of hell, the gates of hell are open, and its walls broken down. Through his sufferings Christ has destroyed hell. Since his resurrection from his hellish death on the cross there is no longer any such thing as 'being damned for all eternity.'[16]

But you say that they know nothing of God's grace and love and frankly are bored with religion. Can they possibly grow and learn? Let me use a husband and wife for an example. The husband loves football. He can sit and watch games and get absolutely absorbed in them. She can't stand them. She doesn't know all this stuff about football. She is bored with all of that. But is there not a possibility that she can be taught and learn about football and maybe even enjoy it? Maybe her husband through his love can draw her into liking football. Only time and love can tell.

Rob Bell in his bold book, *Love Wins,* believes that God's inexpressible love is so powerful that the hardness of the human heart will ultimately respond in a positive way to the unrelenting, infinite expansive love of God. To the question which is stronger human rejection or God's love, Bell contends that love wins. Love never ultimately fails.[17] I believe that the desire of God is that all be saved. The mercy of God according to the Bible is everlasting. God's love never fails.

Our Evangelistic Charge

Well, some might ask, would this not lessen our evangelistic and missionary purposes, if this were true?" I personally think not. Our goal is not to save people from hell but to bring them into fellowship with God. This relationship begins in this world. Our call is to bring people to meet the living God today and to begin a joyous union with the Creator. Why would I want to delay that? Our faith, I believe, is based on love and not fear.

A Call to Faithfulness

In response to Christ, we are called to faithfulness. Revelation warned the early Christians about the persecution from the Roman government. They were warned not to worship the emperor. They were challenged to be faithful unto death. The book of Revelation warned them of things that might happen if they were not faithful. Like these early Christians, we are called to tell others about Christ and follow him faithfully.

Trust God

I don't know about you, but I believe that God is just and good. I believe that God desires the highest and the very best for his creation. God so loved humanity that God sent his son. I do not believe that God's judgment is vindictive or arbitrary. I believe that God's love is based on justice, love and grace. I will trust God to judge and I will seek to prepare myself to be as open and as responsive to God as I can in the light of the revelation I have seen in Jesus Christ our Lord.

5

HEAVEN: THE UNDISCOVERED COUNTRY

A woman poured her heart out to me as she struggled with her grief at her husband's death in a tragic automobile accident. Heartbroken, she sobbed uncontrollably and asked repeatedly, "Why? Why? Where was God?" We talked for some length about our Christian hope of life beyond death. She was a woman who liked to have clear statements and positive evidence to back up what a person said or believed. As a Christian, she wanted to believe that there was life beyond this one, but she asked through her tears, "If there is a future life of some kind after death, why doesn't God write it plainly across the sky?"

If we are honest, we have all felt that way at some point or we will one day. We all long for certainty. But, I don't think we can have it about such matters. I have always been troubled by those persons who seemed to think they have all the answers about heaven, hell and life after death. I am also disturbed by those who deny any possibility of life after death and assert their belief with absolute assurance without any evidence for that opinion. Jeffrey Burton Russell, emeritus professor of history at the University of California, Santa, Barbara, has written a book, *Paradise Mislaid: How We Lost Heaven and How We Can Regain It* (New York: Oxford University Press, 2006), which focuses on the declining belief in heaven in our society today. I believe the Christian is challenged to affirm and seek to understand one's belief in life beyond death. The more I have studied and matured through the years, the more aware I am of the impossibility of anyone having the final or only answer to describe what life will be like after death. But I still believe that life does go on after death. The "heavenly" realm lies before us as an "undiscovered country," and it is always beyond our sure grasp, graphic description, materialistic perspective, intellectual interpretation and human projections. As the Apostle Paul reminds us, "We see through a glass dimly."

Nevertheless, we as Christians, and others affirm our strong faith in life after death. Our hope is based on Paul's confirmation that Jesus "brought life and immortality to light through the gospel" (2 Timothy 1:10). We draw upon Jesus' promise that "I go to prepare a place for you" (John 14:2). The Apostle's Creed affirms that we believe in "the resurrection of the dead" and "the life everlasting."

Can We Contact The Dead?

Without question, we as Christians affirm our faith in life after death, but how do we know? Is there any way we can prove that life continues beyond the grave? Do we have any evidence for such a belief? There are several groups that believe that they have proof of survival after death. Let us look briefly at a few.

Spiritualism

Persons like Edgar Cayce, Jess Stearn, James Van Praagh and Leslie Weatherhead believe that it is possible to commune with the dead. A recent book by Van Praagh, *Talking to Heaven: A Medium's Message of Life and Death* (New York: Penguin Putnam, Inc., 1999), set forth in detail the author's claim to have communicated with the dead. In the Old Testament there is a story where Saul seeks out the spiritualist of Endor (I Samuel 28:8ff) to see if he can contact the dead. Some interpret Jesus' transfiguration and his conversation with Moses and Elijah to be this type of experience (Matthew 17:1-8). Unfortunately, there has been a great amount of deceit, quackery and plain nonsense espoused by these who often advocate spiritualism. Duke University has been involved for some years now to determine whether there is any validity to spiritualism, the psychic dimension, parapsychology and extrasensory perception. Many remain skeptical about spiritualism and dismiss it.

Reincarnation

Put simply, reincarnation is the belief that a person may have lived here on earth in another time and body and may come back to earth several times. Many poets, philosophers, and Christian writers have shared this belief including, Plato, Cicero, Seneca, Walt Whitman, Longfellow, Rudyard Kipling, Rossetti, Browning, Tennyson, Raynor Johnson, C.G. Jung, W. Macnille Dixon, and Leslie Weatherhead. The Christian minister, Leslie Weatherhead believes that reincarnation accounts for the geniuses and child prodigies.[1] In several of his books he sets forth evidence for his belief.[2]

Advocates of this view refer to New Testament passages like Mark 12:24 where Jesus responds to his disciples about whether the blind man's parents sinned or the blind man. The passage seems to state that he sinned in another life. Others say that the response of the disciples to Jesus' question, "Who do men say I am" is evidence. "Some say John the Baptist, some Elijah, others Jeremiah, or one of the prophets" (Luke 9:8-9). After the transfiguration, the disciples remind Jesus that "Elijah must come first." Jesus responds that "Elijah has already come" (Matthew 17:9-13). This is clear reference to John the Baptist. Is he Elijah reincarnated? These believers think so.

The theologian, John Whale, and many others believe that the idea of reincarnation "is incompatible with the very genius of Christianity and there is not a shred of evidence for this doctrine in the New Testament."[3] Outstanding Christian thinkers have aligned themselves both for and against this view. It seems to me that it is difficult to reconcile reincarnation with the Christian faith, though it is not impossible.

Dreams and Visions

Many find evidence for life after death in dreams or visions they have had of deceased loved ones. I have heard and read many stories of persons who actually make such claims. John Killinger has relayed dreams about seeing his parents after they had died and he also shared a vision a woman in Los Angeles had about her mother who had been dead more than thirty years.

This woman saw a circle of light in her hallway about fifteen inches in diameter near the baseboard ten or twelve feet ahead of her. The extremely bright light was divided equally into 3 segments, one gold, one rose, and the third, bluish green. In the middle of the light, stood her mother dressed in a black dress she made when she was 60 years old. In the circle of light her mother looked 60, not 87, as she was when she died. Her mother looked directly at her daughter, seriously and thoughtfully. The vision lasted several seconds.[4]

Recently, I telephoned a medical doctor in another state whose mother had died. His mother had lived to be 85 years old. She was a committed Christian, an active church member and was always youthful, energetic and doing for others. Several days before she died, she told her grandson that she had a dream and saw her mother who said to her, "Irene, it's time to come home.

I don't know about you but I cannot dismiss the many experiences which people have had. There may not be scientific evidence for life beyond the grave but it is a reassuring pointer. The Bible is filled with stories about God, angels and others communicating to persons through dreams. Can it not be possible that our loved ones can?

Death Experiences

I have personally been in the hospital room with church members and have had them tell me about seeing angels, bright lights, Jesus, a loved one who preceded them in death- a mother, a father, child or spouse, hearing singing or some experience that took the fear of death away from them and then they could "let go" and die peacefully.

Oh, I know, many try to explain those feelings away as ego or fear driven. I, however, can not dismiss them so easily. These experiences have not only comforted the one dying but the family members as well. I, too, have been reassured by them.

Near Death Experiences

Some believe that the strongest "evidence" for belief in life after death comes from the astounding experience of many people who have been clinically dead. These people have told about floating out of their body, seeing and hearing others in the hospital room and traveling through a dark tunnel toward a bright light, feeling a great sense of tranquility and peace and being met by a parent, child, or spouse. Then they were revived and brought back to life. Dr. Raymond Moody, Jr. documents many such cases in his book, *Life After Life*,[5] Leslie Weatherhead, George Ritchie, Elisabeth Kubler-Ross, Raynor Johnson, Karl Osis and others tell similar experiences. "In the absence of firm scientific proof, people frequently ask me (Raymond Moody) what I believe: Are NDEs evidence of life after death? My answer is 'yes'."[6] Don Piper recounts his near death experience after his car was crushed by a semi in his book, *90 Minutes in Heaven* and the book, *Heaven Is for Real*, relates the account of a four year old, Colton Burpo, and his trip after death to Heaven and back.

There are some ministers who reject these findings as "cheap grace" and a substitution for faith. Some scientists, psychiatrists, and psychologists dismiss these experiences as hidden recollections of our own birth experiences. These objections are correct in the fact that we cannot "prove" that life exists after death as we cannot prove that God exists. Nevertheless, I believe strongly in both!

Remember the story of Lazarus and the rich man in hell who asks Abraham if someone can warn his brothers so they would change. "They have Moses and the prophets; let them hear them. No, father Abraham, if one went to them from the dead, they will repent." But Abraham replies, "If they hear not Moses and the prophets, neither will they be persuaded, though one rose from the dead" (Luke 16:29-31). Those who are unmoved by the near-death experiences will not be persuaded, as many in Jesus' day and our own were not persuaded by his resurrection.

Omar Khayyam writes in The Rubáiyát:

Strange, is it not? That of the myriads who
    Before us passed the door of Darkness through,
Not one returns to tell us of the Road,
    Which to discover we must travel too.

Even for those of us who believe in life after death, how can
we possibly describe it? It is almost absurd for anyone to try to
describe the "undiscovered country" to which he or she has not yet
visited. But cannot we get some suggestion, hint, flash of insight,
or pointed word from our Lord and the Scripture? I believe we can.
Nevertheless, we have to remember that much of the descriptions
or insight are derived from poetic and symbolic images reflecting
our material world, especially those drawn from the Book of Revelation.

Reinhold Niebuhr, in his monumental book, *The Nature and
Destiny of Man,* has cautioned us that "it is unwise for Christians
to claim any knowledge of either the furniture of heaven or the
temperature of hell; or to be too certain about any details of the
kingdom of God in which history is consummated."[7] He has also
warned that "the Biblical symbols cannot be taken literally because
it is not possible for finite minds to comprehend that which transcends and fulfills history."[8]

Think with me again about the analogy of an unborn baby.
Inside the mother's body, the baby knows nothing of breathing air
for it is surrounded by fluid. The baby has not seen light because
it dwells in darkness. He or she knows nothing about eating food
or drinking liquid, because its nourishment comes through the
umbilical cord. Most of the sound the baby hears is the beating of
the mother's heart. Unless the baby is a twin or one of several, he
or she lives in isolation. How could one possibly explain to a baby,
if you could, what air, light, food, milk, music, walking, friendship
and love are? All of these are beyond his or her experience. They are
radically different and beyond the baby's comprehension.

I believe heaven will be like that for us. Our words, symbols, thoughts and images are inadequate and barren for an "undiscovered country" beyond our imaginations. Let's try, however, remembering the inadequacy of our efforts.

What Is the Meaning of Heaven?

The Resurrection of the Body

Heaven is the realm or place where the resurrected body will dwell. Paul states clearly in I Corinthians 15:35-50 that flesh and blood cannot inherit the Kingdom of God. The body is transformed—changed—"the perishable puts on the imperishable and the mortal puts on immortality, the corruptible puts on the incorruptible." It is a spiritual body which is the whole person minus the physical body. Our spiritual body enables the continuity of our personality. Paul's analogy of the seed shows the spiritual body arising out of the physical as a tulip growing out of the bulb and is connected to it.

Paul also suggests in 2 Corinthians 4:16ff that our spiritual body is God's gift-our salvation- and God's spirit prepares us within for this new "body." The presence of God's spirit is a guarantee of our full resurrection (Romans 8:11 and II Corinthians 5:5). "We shall be like him; for we shall see him as he is" (I John 3:2).

A Place of Worship

Heaven will be a place where we will worship God in the fullness of God's presence. The recreation of a New Jerusalem- the holy city- will be the realization of a holy city where one can be in fellowship with God. God is making his dwelling place—his tent or tabernacle—with men and women. Just as a New Jerusalem was the dream and ideal of the Jews, the heavenly Jerusalem is the fulfillment of the dreams of all those who have longed to be with God. The New Jerusalem is a reminder that God keeps his promises and that ultimately God's kingdom will come and his will be done. It is, according to John in Revelation, the fulfillment of the dream of all persons for community, security, service and worship in an ideal setting.

A Place of Healing and Restoration

Heaven is a place of healing and restoration. In Revelation 22:2 "the leaves from the tree of life" will be for "the healing of the nations." Many enter the spiritual realm broken in body through years of suffering and pain. Others have experienced mental anguish and terrors. Some have died through accidents, have lost an arm or leg, an eye, been severely burned, killed in battle or torture. Heaven will bring balm to their broken bodies and souls. God's medicine from the leaves of this tree touch not only our bodies but reach into the innermost depths of our being. A leaf plucked by faith from this tree assures us of the touch and presence of the Divine Physician.

John likely drew his image of "the tree of life" from the tree in the Garden of Eden (Genesis 3:6) and Ezekiel (47:12). "And by the river, on the bank thereof, on this side and on that side, shall grow all trees for meat whose leaf shall not fade, neither shall the fruit thereof be consumed: it shall bring forth new fruit according to his months. . . and the fruit thereof shall be for meat, and the leaf thereof for medicine."

A Place of Nourishment

The tree not only provides healing but food in its variety and abundance of fruit. The picture is of a different fruit for each month of the year. Could that be symbolic that no matter what our age, young or old, we are nourished by the Tree of Life? In the New Jerusalem, the Tree of Life, whose fruit had been forbidden to be eaten in the Garden of Eden, is now available at the center of the city for all to eat. The fruit is not for Jews only but for all the nations. The tree of life reminds us that we will be continually nourished by God.

I know we should not take this literally, but is this a hint that we might eat in heaven? Remember Jesus told his disciples at the

Last Supper that the cup they drank was a sign of the new covenant and then he added, "I will no longer drink of the fruit of the vine until that day when I drink it new in the kingdom of God" (Mark 14:25).

A Place For Abundant Life

Heaven is a place where there is abundant life. John depicts the River of Life flowing through the New Jerusalem. The life-giving river flows like a shining crystal fountain from the throne of God. The Psalmist had sung about "the river whose streams made glad the city of God" (Psalm 46:4). Earlier in Revelation John spoke about the Lamb who would guide the martyrs "to springs of living water" (Revelation 7:17). Is the river "the living water" Jesus spoke about to the woman at the well? "Whoever drinks of the water that I give him shall never thirst; but the water I shall give him shall be in him a well of water springing up into everlasting life" (John 4:14).

Eternal Life Begins Now

Heaven is where we participate fully in the eternal life which Jesus has promised to all those who abide in him. The eternal life which Jesus offers is not something that begins after death but begins in this life. "And this is eternal life, to know the only true God, and Jesus Christ whom You have sent" (John 17:3). John says, "In him was life" (John 1:4). "I am come," Jesus says, "that they might have life, and that they might have it abundantly" (John 10:20).

I don't think the primary quality of eternal life is greater length, though it certainly continues, but its rare quality is depth. This depth is realized in communion with God which begins in this world. Eternal life, P. T. Forsyth declares, "is a thing indwelling us, it is not a thing outside that awaits us. It is ourselves in a phase, in a new relation."[9] Jesus said, "He that hears my word and believes on him that sent me, has everlasting life" (John 5:24). In the New Testament eternal life is a present possession, here and now. Because it is eternal, it is lasting.

Remember, no matter how you and I perceive of time, it is not the same with God. God is not bound by time as we are. The final consummation and judgment in God's sight is already a present reality for those who believe in the Son. John's Gospel presents an intermingling of time and eternity. "He who believes in the Son already has eternal life." Through the door of death, we experience the abundant life in Christ which begins in this life. "The real moment of transition to the new order of being," John Baillie declares, "is not the moment of physical death but the moment of spiritual rebirth."[10]

A Litany of Absences

The writer of Revelation has written about streets of gold, gates of pearl and walls adorned with every kind of precious stone- jasper, sapphire, emerald, topaz, amethyst, etc. (Revelation 21:18-21). What can these material images mean in a spiritual realm? I personally believe that John was striving to express the wonder, richness, splendor, and glory of the unspeakable life in the city of God. After using these priceless images, John then expounds a litany of absences to describe life in the heavenly city. He then gives a long, negative list of things absent from heaven.

No Sea

Listen to John as he declares: There will be no sea (Revelation 21:1). To those of us who live near the ocean and love it, we do not understand this phrase. The Jewish people, however, were not sailors and hated and feared the sea. The sea represented the enemy and force of chaos and the evil that opposed the Creator God of the universe. This enemy was no threat in heaven. He did not exist. This fear could be put behind them.

No Misery or Death

There will be no sorrow, tears, pain, crying or death (Revelation 21:4). In these verses John gathers up all the misery and burdens of society and promises that they will not exist in the City of God. Isaiah promised that "I will rejoice in Jerusalem and joy in my people; and the voice of weeping shall be no more heard in heaven, nor the voice of crying" (Isaiah 65:19). "God will annihilate death in victory and wipe away all tears" (Isaiah 25:8). Pain, suffering, and death are still a part of our world today, but the hope of heaven is that these things will pass away.

No Unfaithful Believers

There will be no cowards, unbelievers, polluted, murderess, fornicators, sorcerers, idolaters, and liars (Revelation 21:7-8). These persons that John condemns are the *cowards* in face of danger who choose comfort and safety over their love for Christ. The *unbelievers* are those who have said they believe in Christ but their lives deny it. The *polluted* are those who have become tainted by the sins of society. The *murderers* here are probably those who martyred the early Christians. The *fornicators* were those who lived immoral lives. *Sorcerers* were those who tried to make religion magical and superstitious. *Idolaters* worshipped false gods and *liars* are those who live with falsehood and insincerity. This is not a general condemnation of these kinds of people but refers primarily to Christians who were unfaithful during a time of persecution and a danger to the believers in the first century church.

No Temple

There will be no temple (Revelation 21:22). For John the New Jerusalem had no temple because the whole city itself is a temple. It is filled with the presence of God and the people worship everywhere at any time. It is a Holy of Holies, because where God is, there is the church.

No Night, Sun or Moon

There will be no night, sun, or moon (Revelation 21:23, 25, 22:5). The City of God needs no other light because God is the light. Night was a frightening time to the ancient people who lived without our modern electricity and night lights. The night was filled with all sorts of evil. In the City of God, God's light has overcome all terrors and evil.

No Curse

There will be no curse (Revelation 22:3). In heaven, John sees humanity as no longer fallen and cursed by sin but redeemed by God's grace and now worshiping the One who saved them. "The pure in heart will see God" (Matthew 5:8).

No Closed Gates

There will be no closed gates (Revelation 21:2-5). Gates are located on the east, north, south, and west, indicating that persons can enter by many roadways into the presence of God. The gates will never be shut by day or night. This affirms that there is not just one way to God. Jesus stands at the doorway of the human heart and knocks inviting anyone to respond. The doors of heaven are open to all who will enter.

According to John, all barriers in Heaven have been removed by God's love, grace and mercy. God's presence and the depth of God's love fills the New Jerusalem, and everyone there can commune with God. Is it possible as C. S. Lewis has written, that the only way to avoid heaven is to remain "hard at work to hear no music, never to look at earth or sky, and (above all) to love no one"?[11]

What Might We Anticipate as We Look Toward Heaven?

God's Dimension

N. T. Wright, a New Testament scholar and former bishop of Durham in the Church of England, argues that heaven is not so much a future dimension or destiny or another locality, but the hidden or ordinary dimension in our lives, which he characterizes as God's space. These two worlds relate and interlock. He projects "heaven" as God's ultimate reign on earth following the resurrection. He draws upon the image from chapter 21 in the book of Revelation, and other scriptures, where the New Jerusalem comes down out of heaven like a bride adorned for her husband and they (Heaven and earth) are wedded as one. The God who made both heaven and earth will in the end join them together. Christians, he believes, are challenged not so much to be striving toward a future realm apart for this world but to be "citizens of the heavenly kingdom" and charged with the responsibility of being God's agents of love going out into the world with that redeeming love to help overcome evil, right wrongs and minister to all who have needs.[12] Drawing on Wright's depiction of heaven as this worldly, Jon Meacham in his article on "Heaven Can't Wait" in *Time* magazine, concludes: "Heaven thus becomes, for now, the reality one creates in the service of the poor, the sick, the enslaved, the oppressed. It is not paradise in the sky but acts of selflessness and love that bring God's sacred space and grace to a broken world suffused with tragedy until, in theological terms, the unknown hour when the world we struggle to piece together is made whole again."[13]

There is no question that John's image of the New Jerusalem is striking and surely alludes to the consummation of God's final plan for humanity, but, in my biblical understanding this image does not disassemble the other New Testament teachings that point to another spiritual dimension beyond this earthy one. Jesus prayed to his Father in heaven, taught his disciples to pray, 'Our Father, who is in heaven," "Thy kingdom come on earth as it is in heaven." No one knows what God's space is like or how its dimension is determined. I leave that to God who makes us a new creation in Christ Jesus. Without question the Christian is charged to be an agent of reconciliation in the world, being Christ to others, but this is not the only or final place for Christian growth or ministry. Even the founder of the "Social Gospel" movement in our country, Walter Rauschenbusch, did not reject the eschatological dimension in our Christian faith but affirmed that "religion is always eschatological." Without question Rauschenbusch challenges the Christian to be engaged in the service of Christ in the present world. "Our labour for the Kingdom here will be our preparation for our participation hereafter."[14] The Christian does not look to the future spiritual dimension as escapism from this world's problems. We acknowledge our Master's summons that we follow him in service for the Kingdom of God.

The heavenly dimension to which Jesus points not only has an ultimate transformation of the earth in some future time, but has a sense of immediacy for one in his or her dying. "Truly I tell you, today you will be with me in paradise," Jesus assured the thief on the cross who asked to be remembered when Jesus came into his kingdom (Luke 23:43). If there is no present heavenly dimension, where did Jesus ascend when he "was carried up into heaven"? (John 20:17; Luke 24:50-53). Jesus indicated to his disciples that "in his father's house there are many dwelling places," (John 14:1) and that he was going to "prepare a place for you. And if I go and prepare a place for you, I will come again and will take you to myself, so that where I am, there you may be also" (John 14:3). Even the Apostle Paul who speaks about the resurrection of the dead (1 Cor. 15:50-58) also speaks about the possibility of his being put to death because of his ministry for Christ, and declares "For me, living in Christ and dying is gain… I do not know which I prefer. I am hard pressed between the two: my desire is to depart and be with Christ, (italics mine) for that is far better; but to remain in the flesh is more necessary for you" (Philippians 1:23-24). I believe that in the teachings of both Jesus and Paul there is a reference to the present and future dimension to the resurrected body of the Christian. It is a part of the mystery of God's sense of time, spirituality, place, body, and the essence of what constitutes eternal life which begins as a present possession for those in Christ (John 10:28; 17:3). The writer of 1 John expresses the truth this way: "God gave us eternal life, and this life is in his Son. Whoever has the Son has life; and whoever does not have the Son does not have life." (1 John 5:11-12).

What then can the Christian anticipate in the spiritual dimension beyond this earthly realm? As I attempt to peer through the "darkened glass," here are some images I perceive.

Begin Where We Leave Off Here

We will begin in the next life, the spiritual life, where we leave off here. Jesus told us, "to lay up for ourselves, treasures in heaven where moth and rust cannot corrupt" (Matthew 6:19-20). Unfortunately, most of us spend too much of our life pursuing, material things. Most of what we invest our lives in cannot be taken as luggage into the heavenly realm. A desire to help others, a striving to divest ourselves of selfishness, love for others, humility, a commitment to Christ and his way, inner peace and joy are some of the items we might pack in our bag for the celestial city.

Some who have sought to prepare themselves spiritually will feel comfortable in the spiritual realm. They have tried to love Christ and others and serve him. Others who have cared nothing for Christ and rejected all moral values and lived with total disregard for others, cannot expect to be near to the presence of the Holy One. Now is the time to prepare.

A Place of Rest

Heaven will be place of rest for those who need it. Many have toiled and labored hard and their body and spirits are tired and they long for rest. The Scriptures declare that in heaven these persons will "rest from their labors; and their works do follow with them" (Revelation 14:13).

> When the day of toil is done,
> When the race of life is run,
> Father, grant thy wearied one
> Rest for evermore.

We all may desire rest and sleep for awhile, but forever? I believe, however, that it is a false view to see heaven as an endless vacation, continuous relaxation, and perpetual playtime or time of retirement.

If all we are ever going to do is play a harp or sleep, frankly that doesn't sound too exciting or like something I would want to do forever. For some of us who can't read music, if I played under someone else's window for a few hundred years, I think they might throw up the window and exclaim, "Please move on!" What some of us may need after awhile or more immediately is an awakening, not more sleep.

John Steinbeck in *East of Eden* addresses this theme:

[Liz] looked forward to Heaven as a place where cloths did not get dirty and where food did not have to be cooked and dishes washed.

> Privately there were some things in Heaven of which she did not quite approve. There was too much singing, and she didn't see how even the Elect could survive for very long the celestial laziness which was promised. She would find something to do in Heaven. There must be something to take up one's time—some clouds to darn, some weary wings to rub with liniment. Maybe collars of the robes needed turning now and then, and when you come right down to it, she couldn't believe that even in Heaven there would not be cobwebs in some corner to be knocked down with a cloth covered broom.[15]

A Place of Continuous Growth

I believe that Heaven will be a state and place of continuous growth and development. I do not believe the Scriptures teach that the Christian will be idle or sleeping for eternity. The Lord who taught in the parable of the talents that the reward for doing a job well was the granting of greater responsibility is the same Lord who invites us to enter into his eternal joy (Matthew 25:14-30). That joy cannot be idleness. If the saints are "reigning forever and ever," (Revelation 11:15) that means they are doing something. I believe God calls us to further growth in heaven. God is not done with us when we first arrive. He's got a lot of growing in us to do yet. "I believe that God will also complete the work that he has begun with a human life. . ." observes Moltmann. "I believe that God's history with our lives will go on after our death, until that completion has been reached in which a soul finds rest."[16]

In this world, something either grows or dies. Growth is essential for life. Our pathway into heaven may take us through a school rather than before a judgment seat. We enter new classes to help us develop higher character, a more loving and compassionate spirit, deeper humility, patience, self control, love and other virtues. Maybe we can study under the great theologians of all time, Paul, Augustine, Luther, Calvin, Schweitzer, Barth, Bruner, Tillich, or Rauschenbusch. Maybe we can study music under Bach, Beethoven, Mozart, or Mendelssohn. Or perhaps we will study poetry under Tennyson, Blake, Shakespeare, or Longfellow or science under Spinoza, Newton, Einstein, Van Braun, or Niels Bohr. You see what I mean? We have an eternity to find new ways to learn and develop ourselves and serve Christ. "His servants will do him service" (Revelation 22:3). In heaven, our highest goal will be to serve God. That will take an eternity to learn to do.

As Jeffrey Burton Russell has observed, heaven is the "essence" of reality.

> Heaven itself cannot be described, but the human concept of heaven can be. Heaven is not dull; it is not static; it is not monochrome. It is an endless dynamic of joy in which one increasingly realizes one's potential in understanding as well as love is filled more and more with wisdom. It is the discovery, sometimes unexpected, of one's deepest self. Heaven is reality itself; what is not heaven is less real. Hell is the contradiction of heaven; it is the absence of reality.[17]

One translation of Jesus' words in John 14, "In my Father's house are many mansions," reads, "In my father's house are many *stations."* As we grow, we advance to the next "station" or stage. Life is a continuous journey of reaching to what we have not yet achieved or been taught. What an exciting adventure awaits us.

A little girl asked her teacher in school one day, "Do I now know as much as I don't know?" None of us will ever know as much as we do not know- even through all of eternity. So, we better get started!

A Place of Fellowship

Heaven will be a place of fellowship with God and others. We will spend an eternity seeking to worship and live in the presence of God and how to relate to and love others. The arms of God are open to all persons- regardless of race, sex, color or education. The heavenly gates are open to all who will enter by faith. No one is excluded. Many of us still have a long journey to travel in loving others.

A woman asked her minister one day if there would be two places in heaven. "Why do you ask?" he asked her. "Well, I couldn't stand to be in the same room in heaven with Mary. She is so un-refined." "Don't trouble yourself with that, Madam," he replied. "Unless you get rid of that pride, you won't be in heaven at all."

Is There Enough Space in Heaven?

Some are concerned about whether or not heaven could possibly contain all the millions of believers who will be there. In the first place, we assume that the spiritual person occupies space. We do not know that and if the spirit does use space, I know that God can provide the necessary space. Look through a microscope at an atom and we are aware that the world is virtually endless in that direction. Look through a telescope at the stars and the universe is virtually without end in that direction, too. Space with God may be radically different than we can imagine. Leslie Weatherhead has reminded us that there are more brain cells in one person's brain at the present moment than all the people in the world. Each cell has a special function and is important. God will provide room for those who love him. I do not question that.

We Will Know Each Other There

I believe that we will know each other there. If we do not have memory of each other, what kind of happiness would that bring? Memory is a distinct part of our being a person. We all know what it is like to be with a loved one who has dementia, or Alzheimer's. We know them and they do not know us. It's sad. That would not be heaven.

Some have asked, "If we can remember, will that not cause us pain, hurt and other negative feelings?" Some of those feelings may be there, and maybe that's why we need our heavenly school to guide us through them to a stage to handle those feelings properly.

We can take comfort and reassurance in Jesus' words to the thief on the cross. "Today, you will be with me in paradise" (Luke 23:43). If they did not recognize one another, why would they want to meet again? In the transfiguration, Jesus knows Elijah and Moses (Matthew 17:3). Paul says, "we will know as we have been known" (1 Corinthians 13:12).

Those who have been through difficult marriages may find Jesus' words in Luke 20:34f- that "we neither marry or are given in marriage in heaven but are like the angels" -of great comfort. Persons who have had good marriages and have established strong loving bonds want to know if they will know each other and have a relationship in heaven. Jesus' reply to the Sadducees was a response to their "trick" question. He affirmed that women were not merely the "property" of men as marriage was often viewed in Jesus' day. Marriage was seen then primarily as a means to a man having a woman who would provide him a family so his line could continue and give to the woman financial support and security.

Jesus' word that there will be no marriage in heaven and we will be like angels means that the physical side of marriage, sex, will not be present, or necessary. But, I do not believe this excludes the bond of love, faithfulness, companionship and spiritual intimacy which has been established through the years that a husband, wife, children or grandchildren and their wider family may have established. I believe that heaven will provide an endless opportunity for this family to participate with one another and with the wider human family in the heavenly "school."

Final Validation

Heaven is the place where we will experience validation. Paul says, "I have fought the good fight, I have finished my course, I have kept the faith: henceforth there is laid up for me a crown of righteousness" (II Timothy 4:6-8). Ironically, at the time Paul was to stand before the Roman government to be judged, he was claiming victory in Christ. He drew on the analogy of the garland wreath awarded to the victor in the Olympic games. This crown, Paul declares, is not for him only but for all who love the Lord and his appearing. The crown is not reserved for great saints like Paul but all faithful Christian servants, great or small, who serve Christ where they are.

I do not believe that we serve Christ to be rewarded. That would make our motive selfish. I think our desire should be to receive the words, "Well done, my good and faithful servant, enter into the joy I have prepared" (Matthew 25:24).

When we seek to understand Heaven, we remember the words of Paul that "we see through a mirror dimly but then face to face. Now I know in part, then I shall understand fully, ever as I have been fully understood (I Corinthians 13:15). "Heaven is not to be pictured," George Ruther observes, "but entered. We are not dealing with a mural but with a window."[18]

"What no eye has seen nor ear heard, nor the heart of man conceived what God has prepared for those who love him" (I Corinthians 2:9). In quiet confidence, let's trust in the Lord. "In sum, we are called to be on hand for that which is at hand, but not in hand," Christopher Morse, relates, "an unprecedented glory of not being left orphaned but of being loved in a community of new creation beyond all that we can ask or imagine."[19]

The noted Scottish theologian, John Baillie, relates a story about a dying man who was informed by his devotedly Christian doctor that the end was very near. The frightened man asked the doctor if he had any conviction as to what awaited him in the life beyond. The doctor fumbled a moment for an answer. But before he could speak, he heard a scratching at the door. At that moment his answer came to him. "Do you hear that?" the doctor asked the patient. "That is my dog. I left him downstairs, but he grew impatient and has come up and hears my voice. He has no notion what is inside that door, but he knows I am here. Now is it not the same with you. You do not know what lies beyond the Door, but you know your Master is there!"[20]

Our Master is there and that is enough assurance for us. We can trust him, although we do not know the details about "the undiscovered country."

I don't know what picture you have of life after death, but I don't think it should be a picture of idleness. Most of us would certainly not like to sit around and do nothing forever. I think the words of Rudyard Kipling describe something of what life might be beyond death.

> When Earth's last picture is painted
> and the tubes are twisted and dried,
>> When the oldest colors have faded,
>>> And the youngest critic has died,
>> We shall rest and faith, we shall need it—
>>> Lie down for an aeon or two,
>> Till the Master of All Good Workmen
>>> Shall put us to work, anew.
>> And those that were good shall be happy;
>>> They shall sit in a golden chair;
>> They shall splash at a ten-league canvas
>>> With brushes of comet's hair,
>> They shall find real saints to draw from
>>> Magdalene, Peter and Paul:
>> They shall work for an age at a sitting

And never be tired at all!
And only the Master shall praise us,
        And only the Master shall blame;
And no one shall work for money,
        And no one shall work for fame,
But each for the joy of the working
        And each in his separate star,
Shall draw the Thing as he sees It
        For the God of Things as they are!

ENDNOTES

Chapter 1, The Mystery of Death: Behind the Veil

1   Leo Tolstoy, *A Confession and What I Believe*, trans. Aylmer Maude (London: Oxford University Press, 1921), 23-24.

2   Frederick W. Robertson, *Sermons Preached at Brighton* (New York: Harper & Brothers, n.d.), 418.

3   Nicolas Berdyaev, *The Destiny of Man* (New York: Harper Torch books, 1960), 252.

4   Helmut Thielicke, *How the World Began*, trans. John W. Doberstein (Philadelphia: Fortress Press, 1961), 177-178.

5   Albert Schweitzer, *Reverence for Life*, trans. Reginald H. Fuller (New York: Harper & Row, 1969), 69.

6   Jürgen Moltmann, *Theology of Hope* (New York: Harper & Row, 1967), 165.

7   Wolfhart Pannenberg, *The Apostle's Creed in the Light of Today's Questions* (Philadelphia: The Westminster Press, 1972), 97.

8   Gerd Lüdemann, *What Really Happened to Jesus*, (Louisville: Westminster John Knox Press, 1995), 1.

See also Charles Austin Perry, *The Resurrection Promise* (Grand Rapids: William B. Eerdmans Co. 1986)., Morton Kelsey, *Resurrection: Release From Oppression* (New York: Paulist Press, 1985), Pheme Perkins, *Resurrection: New Testament Witness and Contemporary Reflection* (Garden City: Doubleday and Co., 1984), John Shelby Spong, *Resurrection: Myth or Reality?* (San Francisco: Harper Collins, 1994).

9   Moltmann, op. cit., 166.

10   Carlyle Marney, *Faith in Conflict* (New York: Abingdon Press, 1957), 138.

11   Leander E. Keck, "New Testament Views of Death," in *Perspectives on Death*, edited by Liston O. Mills (New York: Abingdon Press, 1969), 97.

12   Paul Tillich, *The Shaking of the Foundations* (New York: Charles Scribner's Sons, 1948), 159.

13   Lewis Mumford, *The Transformation of Man* (New York: Collier Books, 1956), p. 24.

14   Paul Tillich, *The Shaking of the Foundations*, 83.

15   Douglas John Hall, *Professing the Faith* (Minneapolis: Fortress Press, 1993), 358.

16   Emil Brunner, *The Christian Doctrine of the Church, Faith, and the Consummation, Dogmatics, vol. III*, trans. David Cairns (Philadelphia: The Westminster Press, 1960), 386.

17   Frank Stagg, *New Testament Theology* (Nashville: Broadman Press, 1962), 73.

18   H. Wheeler Robinson, *The Religious Ideas of the Old Testament* (London: Gerald Duckworth & Co., LTD, 1959), 85.

19   Douglas John Hall, *God and Human Suffering*, (Minneapolis: Augsburg Publishing House, 1986).

20   Jürgen Moltmann, *The Coming of God*, (Minneapolis: Fortress Press, 1996), 65.

21   John Baillie, *And the Life Everlasting* (New York: Charles Scribner's Sons, 1933), 163.

22   Stagg, op. cit., 326.

23   Emil Brunner, *Eternal Hope*, trans. Harold Knight (London: Lutterworth Press, 1954), 152.

24   Karl Barth, *The Resurrection of the Dead*, trans. H. J. Stenning (New York, Fleming H. Revell Co., 1933), 169.

25   Brunner, *The Christian Doctrine of the Church*, 389.

Chapter 2, The Last Judgment: How God Sizes Us Up

1   Dale Aukerman, *Reckoning With Apocalypse* (New York: Crossroad, 1993), 113.

2   R. Kirby Godsey, *When We Talk About God, Let's Be Honest* (Macon: Smyth and Helwys, 1996), 203.

3   Jürgen Moltmann, *The Coming of God* (Minneapolis: Fortress Press, 1996), 255.

Chapter 3, The Second Coming of Christ: Christ Came and Comes

1 Tim LaHaye and Jerry Jenkins, *Left Behind* (Wheaton: Tyndale House Publishers, 1996) See my book, *The Left Behind Fantasy: The Theology Behind the Left Behind Tales* (Eugene, Oregon: Wipf & Stock Publishers, 2010) for various interpretations of the end times and apocalyptic literature.

2 See Hal Lindsey, *The Rapture* (New York: Bantam Books, 1983); Stephen Travis, *I Believe in the Second Coming* (Grand Rapids: Eerdman Publishing Co., 1982).

3 Albert Schwietzer, *The Quest For The Historical Jesus* (New York: The Macmillan Co. 1961), 228ff.

4 See Darrell L. Bock (editor) *Three Views on the Millennium and Beyond* (Grand Rapids: Zondervan, 1999); Raymond F. Bulman, *The Lure of the Millennium: The Year 2000 and Beyond* (Mary Knoll: Orbis Books, 1999); Frederic J. Baumgarten, *Longing For the End* (New York: St. Martin's Press, 1999); N. T. Wright, *The Millennium Myth.* (Louisville: Westminster/John Knox Press, 1999); Charles L. Feinberg, *Millennialism: The Two Views* (Winona Lake, Indiana: BMH Books, 1985); Damian Thompson, *The End of Time* (London: Sinclair Stevenson, 1996); Dale MacPherson, *The Great Rapture Hoax* (Fletcher, North Carolina: NPI, 1983); Malcolm Bull (editor), *Apocalypse Theory and the End of the World* (Oxford: Blackwell, 1995); Richard Abanes, *End-Time Visions* (Nashville: Broadman and Holman Publishers, 1988). Richard Bauckham and Trevor Hart, *Hope Against Hope: Christian Eschatology at the Turn of the Century* (Grand Rapids: William E. Eerdmans Co., 1999); John Polkingherne and Michael Welker (editors), *The End of the World and the Ends of God* (Harrisburg, Pennsylvania: Trinity Press, 2000); Tim Lahaye and Jerry Jenkins, *Are We Living in the End Times?* (Wheaton: Tyndale House, 1999); William E. Hull, "Left Behind",

Christian Ethics Today, (August, 2001); "Millennialism", *Review & Expositor*, (Summer 2000); "The Bible & The Apocalypse", *Time*, (July 1, 2002).

5   R. Kirby Godsey, *When We Talk About God, Let's Be Honest* (Macon: Smyth & Helwys, 1996). 199.

6   John A. T. Robinson, *Jesus and His Coming* (London: SCM Press, 1957) p. 185.

7   Jürgen Moltmann, *The Coming of God* (Minneapolis: Fortress Press, 1996), p. 202.

8   N. T. Wright, *The Millennium Myth* (Louisville: Westminster/John Knox Press, 1999), 109.

Chapter 4, Hell:Vindictive or Remedial?

1   See "Hell Hath No Fury," *U. S. News and World Report* (January 21, 2000), 45-50.

2   Piero Campones, *The Fear of Hell* (Pennsylvania State University Press, 1991).

3   Emil Bruner, *I Believe in the Living God* (Philadelphia: The Westminster Press, 1951), 81-82.

4   Nels F. S. Ferré, *The Christian Understanding of God* (New York: Harper and Brothers, 1951), 229.

5   C. S. Lewis, *The Problem of Pain* (London: Collins, 1957), 110.

6   Ibid., 116

7   Robert L. Short, *On the Bible and Peanuts* (Louisville: Westminster/John Knox Press, 1990), 127.

8   Jonathan L. Kvanvig, *The Problem of Hell* (New York: Oxford University Press, 1993), 164.

9   Ferré, *The Christian Understanding of God*, 241.

10 Molly T. Marshall, *Trinitarian Soundings* (Shawnee, KS: Central Baptist Theological Seminary, 2011), 45.

11 Dale Moody, *The Word of Truth* (Grand Rapids: William B. Eerdmans Publishing Company, 1981), 496.

12 George William Ruther, *The Four Last Things* (Evanston: Credo House, 1980), 146.

13 Walter Rauschenbusch, *A Theology for The Social Gospel* (New York: The Macmillan Co., 1917), 215.

14 Ibid., 234

15 John Hick, *Evil and The God of Love* (New York: Harper and Row, 1966), 379.

16 Jürgen Moltmann, *The Coming of God* (Minneapolis: Fortress Press, 1996), 253-254. See also John Benton, *How Can a God of Love Send People To Hell?* (Welwyn, Hertfordshire: Evangelical Press, 1985); Alan E. Bernstein, *The Formation of Hell* (Ithaca: Cornell University Press, 1993). See also Francis Chan and Preston Sprinkle, *Erasing Hell: What God Said about Eternity, and the Things We Have Made Up* (Elgin, IL: David C. Cook, 2011), Edward William Fudge, *The Fire that Consumes: A Biblical and Historical Study of the Doctrine of Final Punishment* (Eugene, Oregon: Wipf and Stock, 2011), and Edward William Fudge, *Hell A Final Word: The Surprising Truths* (Abilene, Texas: Leafwood Publishers 2012).

17 Rob Bell, *Love Wins* (New York: HarperOne, 2010), 109.

Chapter 5, Heaven: The Undiscovered Country

1 Leslie A. Weatherhead, *The Christian Agnostic* (New York: Abingdon Press, 1965), 299ff.

2 See Weatherhead, *Life Begins at Death* and *Wounded Spirits*.

3 J. S. Whale, *The Christian and the Problem of Evil* (London: SCMP Press, 1957), 55.

4 John Killinger, *You Are What You Believe* (Nashville: Abingdon Press, 1990), 116-117.

5 Raymond A. Moody, Jr. *Life After Life* (New York: Bantam Books, 1976).

6 Raymond A. Moody, Jr. *The Light Beyond* (New York: Bantam Books, 1988), 154. See also Don Piper, *90 Minutes in Heaven* (Grand Rapids, Michigan: Revell, 2004) and Todd Burpo, *Heaven Is for Real* (Nashville: Thomas Nelson, 2010).

7 Reinhold Niebuhr, *The Nature and Destiny of Man*, vol. II (New York: Charles Scribner's Sons, 1949), 294.

8 Ibid., 289.

9 P. T. Forsyth, *This Life and the Next* (Boston: The Pilgrim Press, 1948), 55.

10 John Baillie, *And the Life Everlasting* (New York: Charles Scribner's Sons, 1933), 249.

11 C. S. Lewis, *Till We Have Faces* (London: William Collins Sons & Co. 1956), 80-84.

12 N. T. Wright, *Surprised by Hope: Rethinking Heaven, the Resurrection, and the Mission of the Church* (New York: HarperOne, 2008), 104-108,114-117,148-151. . See also *How God Became King: The Forgotten Story of the Gospels* (New York: HarperOne, 2012).

13 Jon Meacham, "Heaven Can't Wait: Why Rethinking the Hereafter Could Make the World a Better Place," *Time* (April 16, 2012) vol. 179, No. 15, 32-33.

14 Walter Rauschenbusch, *A Theology for the Social Gospel* (New York: The Macmillan Company, 1917), 239.

15 John Steinbeck, *East of Eden* (New York: The Viking Press, 1952), Chapter XXIV.

16 John Polkingherne and Michael Welker (editors) *The End of the world and the Ends of God* (Harrisburg, Pennsylvania: Trinity Press, 2000), 252.

17 Jeffrey Burton Russell, *A History of Heaven: The Singing Silence* (New Jersey: Princeton University Press, 1997), pp. 4-5. See also Jeffrey Burton Russell, *Paradise Mislaid: How We Lost Heaven and How We Can Regain It* (New York: Oxford University Press, 2006).

18 George William Ruther, *The Four Last Things* (Evanston: Credo House, 1986), p. 191. For further reading see Collen McDannell and Bernhard Long, *Heaven: A History* (New Haven: Yale University Press, 1988); *The Book of Heaven* edited by Carol Zaleski and Philip Zaleski (New York: Oxford Press, 2000); J. Edward Wright, *The Early History of Heaven* (New York: Oxford, 2000); *The End of the World and the Ends of God*, edited by John Polkingherne and Michael Welker (Harrisburg, Pennsylvania: Trinity Press, 2000). Jay D. Robison, *Life After Death: Christian Interpretations of Personal Eschatology* (New York: Peter Lang, 1998); Peter Toon, *Heaven and Hell: A Biblical Overview* (Nashville: Abingdon, 1986), and N. T. Wright, *Surprised by Hope: Rethinking Heaven, the Resurrection and the Mission of the Church* (Grand Rapids, Michigan: Zondervan, 2010). See also Jon Meacham, "Heaven Can't Wait: Why Rethinking the Hereafter Could Make the World a Better Place," *Time*, vol. 179, No. 15, (April 18, 2012), 30-36. William H. Willimon, *Who Will Be Saved?* (Nashville: Abingdon Press, 2008), and Paul Dafydd Jones, "A Hopeful Universalism," *The Christian Century*, (June 27, 2012).

19 Christopher Morse, *The Difference Heaven Makes* (London: T. & T. Clark, 2010), 121.

20 John Baillie, *And the Life Everlasting*, 237-238.

ALSO FROM ENERGION PUBLICATIONS

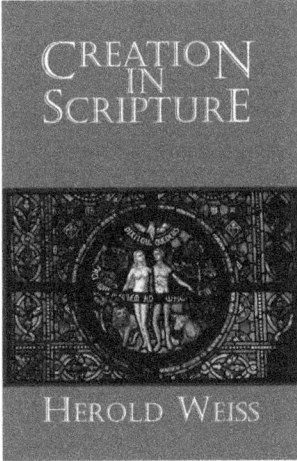

What a remarkable little book: at once a bold challenge to creationism, exposing its reactionary impulses and indicting its ideological abuses of the Bible; and, at the same time, a generous invitation for thoughtful Christians to celebrate the amazingly rich and varied portraits of creation, and thereby to bolster their faith in the Creator in a way that is both well-conceived and biblically based.

Terence J. Martin, Ph.D.
Professor of Religious Studies
St. Mary's College, Notre Dame

ALSO BY THE AUTHOR

This is a serious book about a subject we focus on all too seldom these days — the power and the meaning of the Cross of Christ. I'm glad to say it warmed my heart. I think it will warm yours as well.

John Killinger
Professor, pastor, and author of 50 books, including *The Changing Shape of Our Salvation*

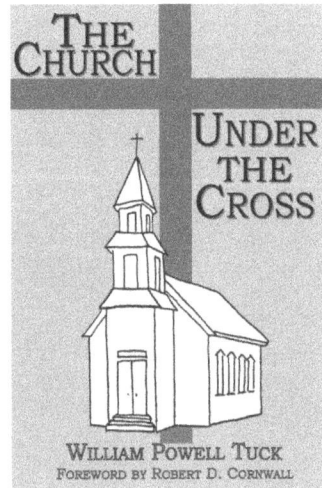

More from Energion Publications

Personal Study

Finding My Way in Christianity	Herold Weiss	$16.99
Holy Smoke! Unholy Fire	Bob McKibben	$14.99
The Jesus Paradigm	David Alan Black	$17.99
When People Speak for God	Henry Neufeld	$17.99
The Sacred Journey	Chris Surber	$11.99

Christian Living

Faith in the Public Square	Robert D. Cornwall	$16.99
Grief: Finding the Candle of Light	Jody Neufeld	$8.99
I Want to Pray	Perry M. Dalton	$7.99
Soup Kitchen for the Soul	Renee Crosby	$12.99
Crossing the Street	Robert LaRochelle	$16.99

Bible Study

Learning and Living Scripture	Lentz/Neufeld	$12.99
From Inspiration to Understanding	Edward W. H. Vick	$24.99
Luke: A Participatory Study Guide	Geoffrey Lentz	$8.99
Philippians: A Participatory Study Guide	Bruce Epperly	$9.99
Ephesians: A Participatory Study Guide	Robert D. Cornwall	$9.99

Theology

Creation in Scripture	Herold Weiss	$12.99
Creation: the Christian Doctrine	Edward W. H. Vick	$12.99
The Politics of Witness	Allan R. Bevere	$9.99
Ultimate Allegiance	Robert D. Cornwall	$9.99
History and Christian Faith	Edward W. H. Vick	$9.99
The Church Under the Cross	William Powell Tuck	$11.99

Ministry

Clergy Table Talk	Kent Ira Groff	$9.99
Out of This World	Darren McClellan	$24.99

Generous Quantity Discounts Available
Dealer Inquiries Welcome
Energion Publications — P.O. Box 841
Gonzalez, FL_ 32560
Website: http://energionpubs.com
Phone: (850) 525-3916

www.ingramcontent.com/pod-product-compliance
Lightning Source LLC
Chambersburg PA
CBHW031600040426

42452CB00006B/365